UKRAINE
Waldkarpaten
Dnjestr
Pruth
Kischinau
MOLDAWIEN
UKRAINE
www.kartographie.de
25 km
N
KEI
es Erzgebirge
dapest
ARN
Ungarische Tiefebene
Theiß
Ostkarpaten
Siebenbürgen
RUMÄNIEN
Mureş (Mieresch)
Südkarpaten
Galati
Izmail
Sulina
Braila
Donau
Walachei
Dobrudscha
Constanta
Vukovar
Novi Sad
Donau
Belgrad
Eisernes Tor
Drobeta-Turnu Severin
Olt (Alt)
Bukarest
Silistra
Russe
Vidin
Warna
SERBIEN
Drina
Morava
Westbalkan
BULGARIEN
Ostbalkan
Hoher Balkan
Schwarzes Meer
Sofia
MONTE-NEGRO
KOSOVO

Jutta Gay

Die Donau

Von der Quelle bis zur Mündung

The Danube

From the source to the delta

Autorin: Jutta Gay, Köln
Übertragung ins Englische: Linda Marianiello & Tammi Reichel
für APE Int'l, LLC, Richmond
Gesamtproducing: Hans-Joachim Schneider, Jutta Gay
Gesamtherstellung: KOMET Verlag GmbH, Köln

ISBN 978-3-89836-966-4

www.komet-verlag.de

Jutta Gay

Die Donau

Von der Quelle bis zur Mündung

The Danube

From the source to the delta

KOMET

Inhalt

Contents

Vorwort

Donaueschingen. Ein kleines Städtchen am Rande der Schwäbischen Alb, das im Jahr nicht viele Besucher sehen würde, hätte es nicht eine kleine Besonderheit zu bieten: die Quelle der Donau. Nichts sprudelt hier wild und unbändig, wie man es vielleicht erwarten würde; stattdessen quillt reines, klares Wasser ganz ruhig aus dem tiefen Karstgestein der Alb in ein kleines Bassin. Hier also entspringt die mächtige Donau, die sich laut einer Tafel auf nunmehr 2840 Flusskilometern durch halb Europa windet und sich auf ihrem Weg zum zweitlängsten Strom des Kontinents entwickelt?

Das kann man sich vielleicht kaum vorstellen und mag streng wissenschaftlich auch nicht ganz richtig sein, aber wir nehmen dennoch auf einer der Steinbänke Platz und erfreuen uns an dem schönen Bild: Das stille Wasser spiegelt die fürstliche Schlosskapelle Sankt Johann, und eine allegorische Figurengruppe zeigt dem Besucher, in welche Richtung sich der Fluss von nun an seinen Weg bahnt – nach Osten, durch zehn Länder und unzählige Landschaften hindurch, stetig dem Schwarzen Meer entgegenströmend, in das er zuletzt in einem weiten Delta mündet.

Foreword

Donaueschingen is a small town on the edge of the Swabian Alb mountains. This sleepy spot would probably not see too many visitors if not for one unique feature: the source of the Danube River. There is no wild, unrestrained bubbling water here, as one might expect. Instead, pure, clear water flows peacefully out of the deep limestone rock of the mountains into a small pool. Can this be the same mighty Danube that flows on and meanders through half of Europe, its course extending 2,840 km (1,764 miles), according to a plaque, to become the second longest river on the European Continent?

That may be hard to imagine, and from a strictly scientific standpoint may not be entirely accurate. Even so, we'll take a seat on a stone bench nearby to appreciate the beautiful setting. The still water mirrors the splendid Church of St. John the Baptist. An allegorical group of statues shows visitors the direction the river wends its way from here on: she heads eastward, passing through ten countries and countless landscapes, moving steadily toward the Black Sea, where she finally empties into the sea in an expansive delta.

▲ Die Donauquelle der Herzen: der Quelltopf in Donaueschingen
▲ The popular and traditional source of the Danube: a spring at the castle in Donauseschingen

Die Quellen der Donau - Anfang und Ende eines Flusses

Der Streit um den Ursprung der Donau währt bereits seit Jahrhunderten. Aristoteles etwa vermutete ihre Quelle in den Pyrenäen, Herodot irgendwo in Spanien. Doch während für die antiken Völker die Quellen im Barbarenland eine terra incognita waren, die es noch zu erobern und zu erforschen galt, ist der Streit der vergangenen Jahrhunderte der zwischen zwei deutschen Städtchen, die beide die Donauquelle für sich beanspruchen wollen.

So viel ist mittlerweile sicher: Die Donau entspringt in der Baar, einer sanft hügeligen, fruchtbaren Landschaft am Rande von südlichem Schwarzwald und Schwäbischer Alb, die von tiefem Karstgestein geprägt ist. Überall sickern dort kleine Quellen aus dem Boden, die entweder bald darauf wieder ver-

The Sources of the Danube - Where the River Begins and Ends

The dispute over the origin of the Danube has gone on for centuries. Aristotle, for example, thought its source was in the Pyrenees, while Herodotus imagined it to be somewhere in Spain. For people of the ancient world, the Danube's sources in barbarian lands were terra incognita, places that had yet to be conquered and explored. During more recent centuries, however, the quarrel has centered around two German cities, both of which would like to lay claim to its source.

This much is certain by now: the Danube arises in the Baar, a region of gentle hills and fertile land on the edge of the southern Black Forest and the Swabian Alb that is characterized by deep limestone rock formations. Everywhere, little springs bubble up from the ground and either seep back into the

▲ Mutter Baar weist der jungen Donau den Weg nach Osten.
▲ Mother Baar shows the young Danube the way eastward.

sickern oder kleine Bäche bilden. Drei davon, Brigach, Breg und Donaubach – und vermutlich ein halbes Dutzend weiterer Rinnsale –, vereinigen sich später zur Donau, wobei Furtwangen für die Breg und Donaueschingen für den Donaubach für sich auch jeweils die Hauptquelle des Flusses anmelden.

Betrachtet man das Thema rein emotional, so geht Donaueschingen ganz klar als Sieger aus dem Quellenstreit hervor: Deutlich mehr Besucher besichtigen den Quelltopf des Donaubaches, den die Grafen von Fürstenberg, die dort seit 1353 residieren, zwischen ihrem Schloss und der Kirche Sankt Johann prachtvoll in Marmor und Sandstein einfassen ließen. Von einer steinernen Balustrade und Bänken umrahmt, zeigt sich im Schlosspark ein beschauliches Bild: Das klare Wasser der sogenannten Karst-Ausstoßquelle schimmert im Strom einiger Wasserpflanzen grünlich, und am Grund blinkt die ein oder andere Münze hervor. Viele Besucher werfen, in der

ground or form small streams. Three of these, the Brigach, the Breg, and the Danube stream (and presumably a half-dozen other rivulets), later merge into the Danube River. That's why Furtwangen makes a claim for the Breg, and Donaueschingen for the Danube stream, as the river's main source.

From a purely emotional standpoint, Donaueschingen is the clear winner in the dispute over the source. There are considerably more visitors to the source of the Danube stream, which the counts of Fürstenberg, who have resided here since 1353, had enclosed in a splendid basin of marble and sandstone situated between their palace and the Church of St. John the Baptist. Surrounded by a stone balustrade and benches, the Danube spring is a contemplative spot on the palace grounds. Clear water from what is known as the karst "ejection source" shimmers with the green of several water plants, and here and there a coin sparkles on the bottom.

▲ Den langen Weg der Donau bis zur Mündung zeigt eine ungarische Gedenktafel am Quelltopf in Donaueschingen.
▲ A Hungarian commemorative plaque at the castle spring in Donaueschingen shows the long route of the Danube to its estuary.

Hoffnung, einmal wiederzukommen, ein paar Cent in das Bassin. Daneben, auf reliefverzierten Tafeln, wurden die wichtigsten Eckdaten zur Donau in Stein gehauen: 2840 Kilometer legt das Wasser von Donaueschingen aus zurück, bis es ins Schwarze Meer mündet, 678 Meter liegt die Quelle über dem Meer.

Rund um die Quelle an einer Mauer haben die Anrainerstaaten der Donau Plaketten mit Gedichten und Zitaten zur Donau angebracht, und die Schlosskirche Sankt Johann entfaltet ihre böhmisch-barocke Pracht nicht nur, wenn sie sich im Quelltopf spiegelt: Auch ihr Inneres kann sich sehen lassen und hält einige bedeutende Kunstwerke bereit. Das Fürstenbergische Schloss gleich nebenan ist ebenso sehenswert, enthält es doch eine naturkundliche Sammlung, die vom Leben an und in der Donau zeugt. Doch das Hauptaugenmerk des Besuchers ruht meist auf der allegorischen Figur, welche die Quelle überragt und 1895 von Adolf Heer geschaffen

Many visitors toss a few cents into the basin, hoping to return again some day. Alongside it, the key features of the Danube have been carved in relief on ornamental tablets: the water covers 2,840 km (1,764 miles) from Donaueschingen until it flows into the Black Sea, and the source lies 678 meters (2,224 feet) above sea level.

The states that border the river have mounted plaques bearing poetry and quotes about the Danube on a wall around the spring basin, and the Bohemian-baroque splendor of the Church of St. John the Baptist is evident not only when it is reflected in the castle spring. The interior is also impressive and houses a number of important works of art. The Fürstenberg palace is directly next door and worth seeing; it contains a natural history collection that explores life in and around the Danube. But visitors' attention is mainly drawn to the allegorical figure created by Adolf Heer in 1895 that towers over the source: the Danube is depicted in the form of a young

▲ Ein ganz anderes Bild als das von Donaueschingen eröffnet sich dem Besucher der Bregquelle. 2888 Kilometer liegen vor dem Wasser der Breg, bis es ins Schwarze Meer mündet.
▲ Visitors to the Breg source find an entirely different scene from that in Donaueschingen. About 2,880 km (1,795 miles) lie ahead for the waters of the Breg before they flow into the Black Sea.

wurde: Die Donau erscheint hier als junges Mädchen, die von „Mutter Baar" auf den Weg nach Osten geschickt wird. Folgen kann man dem Bächlein zunächst nicht – unterirdisch fließt es durch den der Öffentlichkeit nicht zugänglichen Fürstenbergischen Schlosspark, an dessen Ende es erst wieder zutage tritt.

Ein ganz anders Bild zeigen dagegen die Quelle der Breg und ihre Umgebung: Nördlich von Furtwangen an einer kleinen Marienkapelle findet sich hier eine Einfassung, der man weit weniger als der in Donaueschingen zutraut, einen solchen Fluss hervorzubringen. Das Rinnsal, das sich den Hügel hinab Richtung Donaueschingen begibt, wirkt zunächst enttäuschend. Hier weist eine Tafel die Breg als Hauptquellfluss der Donau aus. Das ist wissenschaftlich gesehen fundiert, denn die Breg führt wesentlich mehr Wasser zur Donau als der Donaubach und ist auch von der Mündung am Schwarzen Meer am weitesten entfernt, nämlich genau 2888 Kilometer.

girl who is sent on her eastward journey by "Mother Baar." We cannot follow the little brook at first, as it flows underground through the grounds of the Fürstenberg palace, which are not open to the public. The little brook surfaces at the point where the park ends.

The source of the Breg and its surroundings present an entirely different scene. Here, at a little Marian chapel north of Furtwangen, the Breg seems much less likely to give rise to such a mighty river than the Donaueschingen spring. The trickle of water that makes its way downhill toward Donaueschingen is a bit of a disappointment at first. A plaque identifies the Breg as the Danube's main source, and scientifically speaking this is true, since the Breg contributes significantly more water to the Danube River than the Danube stream. It is also farthest from the point where the Danube meets the Black Sea, precisely 2,888 km (1,794.5 miles) away. But there's no need to focus on science at the Breg source

▲ Kaiser Wilhelm II. gab den Bau des Donautempels, der den Donaubach in die Brigach leitet, zu Beginn des 20. Jahrhunderts in Auftrag.
▲ Kaiser Wilhelm II commissioned the building of the Danube Temple where the Danube stream flows into the Brigach in the early twentieth century.

▲ Zahlreiche Schwarzwaldquellen und -bäche speisen Brigach und Breg, bevor diese sich zur Donau vereinigen.
▲ Numerous spring and brooks in the Black Forest feed the Brigach and Breg before they merge into the Danube.

Doch eigentlich sollte man auch an der Bregquelle seine Zeit nicht mit der Wissenschaft vertun, hat man es hier doch mit einer ganz anderen Idylle zu tun als mit der in Donaueschingen: hier die sanften Hügel des Südschwarzwaldes, dort die repräsentative Fürstenbergische Residenz.

Der dritte Quellfluss der Donau, die Brigach, entspringt etwas weiter nördlich in Sankt Georgen im Schwarzwald. Auch ihre Quelle ist eher unspektakulär, doch der Bach mäandert sachte durch das schön bewaldete Brigachtal, schwillt durch das Wasser unzähliger Schwarzwaldquellen immer weiter an und ist bereits ein kleiner Fluss, wenn er Donaueschingen erreicht. Jenseits des Fürstlichen Schlossparks ergießt sich – in einem dünnen Strahl und unter einem griechischen Tempel hervor – der Donaubach in die Brigach. Und nun endlich, ein paar Meter flussabwärts, treffen auch

either, because we're surrounded by a totally different idyll than in Donaueschingen. Here, instead of the impressive Fürstenberg residence, are the rolling hills of the southern Black Forest.

The third source of the Danube, the Brigach, arises somewhat farther north, in Sankt Georgen in the Black Forest. The Brigach source is also rather unspectacular, but the brook gently meanders through the beautifully forested Brigach Valley, swelling as it is joined by countless Black Forest springs along the way. By the time it reaches Donaueschingen, the Brigach is already a little river. On the far side of the noble palace grounds, the Danube stream empties–in a thin jet from beneath a Greek temple–into the Brigach. Finally, just a short way downstream, the Brigach and Breg meet, and the old maxim comes to

Brigach und Breg aufeinander, und der alte Merksatz wird wahr: Brigach und Breg bringen die Donau zu Weg. Ein kleiner grüner Flecken, auf dem Bänke unter Birken einladen, tut sich am Zusammenfluss der Flüsse auf, noch einmal schauen Mutter Baar und die junge Donau in Stein gehauen nach Osten, dem Fluss hinterher.

Von nun an spricht man auch endlich von der Donau; vor ihr liegen 2845 Flusskilometer – und hinter ihr der Quellenstreit, denn Geografen machten diesem ein Ende. Sie begannen die Kilometerzählung statt an der Quelle ganz einfach im rumänischen Donaudelta, in dem sich, nahe der Stadt Sulina, der Donaukilometer 0 befindet. Doch auch diese Berechnung ist mittlerweile nicht mehr ganz aktuell: Durch die von der Donau mitgeführten Schwemmstoffe verschiebt sich die Donaumündung jedes Jahr um einige Kilometer ins Schwarze Meer, und der Nullkilometer findet sich nun einige Kilometer davor im Binnenland.

life: "The Brigach and Breg set the Danube on its way." At the confluence is a little green spot with inviting benches under the branches of beech trees. Mother Baar and the young Danube, carved in stone, once again look downriver.

From this point on, we are truly speaking about the Danube River. She still has almost 2,845 km (1,768 miles) before her, but the debate source is behind her, because geographers have put an end to it. Instead of measuring the river's length beginning at the source, they simply began in the Romanian delta near the city of Sulina, which is the location of the zero kilometer marker for the Danube River. Strangely enough, even this calculation is no longer entirely accurate. Due to the silt the Danube carries along with it, the point where the Danube joins the Black Sea shifts each year. The zero marker is now a few kilometers in the interior.

▾ 2845 Flusskilometer legt die Donau vom Zusammenfluss von Brigach und Breg bis zu ihrem Nullkilometer im rumänischen Sulina zurück.
▾ The Danube River covers a distance of 2,845 km (1,768 miles) from the confluence of the Brigach and the Breg to the zero marker in the Romanian city of Sulina.

Exkurs: Das Antlitz der Donau

Als grimmig-schrecklicher Flussgott Danubius, mit wallendem, zerzaustem Haar und Bart, so wird die Donau in der bildenden Kunst meist dargestellt. Am Vierströmebrunnen auf der Piazza Navona in Rom etwa, ab 1648 von Gian Lorenzo Bernini für Papst Innozenz X. errichtet, erhebt sich die Gottheit als Sinnbild Europas – neben dem Ganges für Asien, dem Nil für Afrika und dem Rio de la Plata für Amerika. Auch in Budapest und Wien präsentieren Brunnenfiguren einen furchtbaren Flussgott und symbolisieren damit die Gewalt, die die Wasser der Donau, ihre Strömungen, Hochwasser und Vereisungen, anrichten können. Doch zeigt der Wiener Danubius auch eine zarte Seite: Sanft hält er Vindobona, die Personifikation Wiens, in seinem Arm, beschützt sie und umschmeichelt sie gleichzeitig. Einzig in Donaueschingen hat die Donau ein ganz anderes Gesicht: Ein unbeschwertes, junges Mädchen ist sie an der Donauquelle, ein Kind sogar auf einem Denkmal am Zusammenfluss von Brigach und Breg. Und dennoch muss auch diese zarte Donau einige Kilometer weiter eine Kraft beweisen, die in Anbetracht ihres wenigen Wassers derjenigen der mächtigen Götter in nichts nachsteht.

Excursion: The Face of the Danube

In the fine arts, the Danube is most often portrayed as the fierce and terrible river god Danubius, with a wild beard and tousled mane of hair. The Fountain of Four Rivers on the Piazza Navona in Rome, for example, was sculpted by Gian Lorenzo Bernini for Pope Innocent X starting in 1648 and depicts Danubius as the symbol of Europe, along with the Ganges for Asia, the Nile for Africa, and the Rio de la Plata for the Americas. Fountains in Budapest and Vienna also contain figures of a fearful river god and symbolize the power of the waters of the Danube–its currents, floods, freezing, and thawing. But the Viennese Danubius also has a tender side; he gently lays an arm around Vindobona, the personification of Vienna, both to protect and to woo her. Only in Donaueschingen does the Danube have an entirely different face. There she is a carefree young girl at the Danube source, a child, even, in the monument at the confluence of Brigach and Breg. But even this gentle Danube must prove her mettle several kilometers further on, and in light of the low volume of water here, her power is in no way inferior to that of the mighty gods.

◄ Der erbarmungslose Danubius am Vierströmebrunnen in Rom und ▼ in Wien am Albrechtsbrunnen

◄ The merciless Danubius is part of the Fountain of Four Rivers in Rome and ▼ the Albrecht Fountain in Vienna.

▼ Ein unschuldiges Kind: die junge Donau im Arm ihrer Mutter an der Mündung der Brigach in die Breg

◄ An innocent child: the young Danube at her mother's knee at the confluence of the Brigach and the Breg

Die deutsche Donau

Sehr gemächlich nimmt die Donau ihre Reise Richtung Schwarzes Meer auf: ein kleiner Fluss, der sich zunächst begradigt, bald aber in weiten, weitgehend natürlichen Schleifen seinen Weg durch eine üppige Wald- und Wiesenlandschaft der Baar bahnt und nach ein paar Kilometern in den Naturpark Obere Donau eintritt. Die Donau hat an Kraft gewonnen – und treibt mit ihr bei Geisingen die erste Mühle an. Die ist bereits seit dem Jahr 1139 in Betrieb und heute an der oberen Donau die einzige noch aktive Mühle. Hier beginnt auch die Schwäbische Alb, durch deren weißes, dicht bewaldetes Jurakalkgestein sich die Donau ein tiefes Bett gegraben hat.

Womit, fragt man sich unweigerlich wenige Kilometer hinter Geisingen bei dem Ort Immendingen, wenn man in hei-

The German Danube

The Danube assumes a very leisurely pace as it sets off in the direction of the Black Sea. It begins as a small river running in a straight line, but soon winds its way through the luxurious Baar landscape of forests and meadows in wide loops, most of them following their natural course. A few kilometers later it enters the Upper Danube Nature Preserve. The Danube has gained strength and now, near Geisingen, powers its first mill. The mill has stood there since 1139, and is the only one still in operation on the Upper Danube. This is also the start of the Swabian Alb mountains, where the Danube has carved a deep bed through its thickly forested, white limestone formations dating from the Jurassic period.

"How is that possible?" people inevitably wonder a few kilometers beyond Geisingen near the town of Immendingen,

▼ Die Kraft der Donau treibt seit 1139 die Mühle von Geisingen an.
▼ The Geisingen Mill has been powered by the Danube since 1139.

▲ Naturpark Obere Donau – eine der schönsten Gegenden Baden-Württembergs
▲ The Upper Danube Nature Preserve, one of the most beautiful spots in Baden-Württemberg

ßen Sommern ganz plötzlich in einem völlig trockenen Flussbett, aber auch nach der Schneeschmelze an einem nach wie vor eher unscheinbaren Flüsschen steht.

Es ist ein Phänomen des unterirdischen Karstgesteins der Alb: Die zerklüfteten Kalksteinschichten sind durch Erdkrustenverschiebungen zerbrochen, bilden in der Tiefe Gänge und Höhlen, schlucken das Donauwasser und leiten es um. Die Donau wird deutlich flacher und schmaler, und in regenarmen oder sehr heißen Zeiten kann man im Flussbett trockenen Fußes spazieren gehen. 1874 war die Donau das erste Mal restlos verschwunden, und man versuchte, die Löcher mit Steinen, Sand und Holz zu verschließen – vergeblich. Man war sich völlig im Unklaren darüber, was mit dem Donauwasser geschah. Bei der Suche nach den Ursachen kam man schließlich auf den Gedanken, das Wasser würde versickern und die 12 Kilometer entfernte Aachquelle – Deutschlands größte Quelle – speisen. Um dies zu beweisen, goss der Geologe

where the riverbed is suddenly dry as a bone in the heat of summer. Even after the spring thaw, you still might find yourself standing by a rather insignificant little stream.

This phenomenon is caused by the underground karst formations of the Swabian Alb. Movements in the earth's crust have caused the craggy limestone layers to break apart, forming deep, underground tunnels and caves that absorb and divert water from the Danube. The Danube becomes markedly flatter and narrower, and in periods of low precipitation or very high temperatures, people can take a dry-footed stroll on the riverbed. The Danube first disappeared without a trace in 1874. People tried to close off the holes with stones, sand and wood, but in vain. They were completely puzzled as to what had happened to the water of the Danube. Searching for the explanation, they finally realized that the water could have seeped into the ground and fed into the Aachtopf, Germany's largest spring, about 12 km (7.5 miles) away. In order to prove

Adolf Knop 1877 Salz, grünen Farbstoff und stinkendes Schieferöl vor die Hauptversinkungsstelle bei Immendingen in die Donau. 60 Stunden später tauchten alle drei Stoffe im Aachtopf wieder auf.

Indem die Donau so die Wasserscheide zwischen Rhein und Donau umgeht, fließt ein Großteil ihres Wassers – über die Aachquelle, die Aach und den Bodensee – letztendlich in den Rhein und damit in die Nordsee. Die Donau selbst muss sich zunächst mit dem wenigen ihr verbliebenen Wasser begnügen, bevor sie sich – von einigen Nebenflüssen versorgt – mit den Kalkfelsen der Alb abmühen darf.

Das Tal der Donau wird schmal: Weiße Felsnadeln sprießen zwischen den dicht bewaldeten Hängen hervor – ein Paradies für Kletterer und die Fauna der Alb. Wenn die Donau

this theory, geologist Adolf Knop poured salt, green dye and stinking shale oil into the Danube at the main spot where the water sank below ground, near Immerdingen. Sure enough, sixty hours later, all three materials reappeared in the Aachtopf.

Due to the way the Danube bypasses the watershed between the Rhine and the Danube, a significant portion of its water flows via the Aachtopf, the Aach River and Lake Constance ultimately into the Rhine River and the North Sea. The Danube itself must make do with what little water remains, supplied by a few tributaries, until she can struggle free of the limestone rock of the Alb.

The Danube Valley becomes narrow: white, rocky pinnacles jut out from the thickly forested slopes. This area is a paradise for climbers and for the fauna of the Alb. When the Danube

▼ 5000 Liter Donauwasser versinken pro Sekunde bei Immendingen – und tauchen etwa 60 Stunden später im Aachtopf wieder auf.
▼ Danube water sinks at this spot near Immendingen at a rate of 5,000 liters (1,320 gallons) per second and reappear sixty hours later in the Aachtopf.

sich in einer weiten Schleife um die Felsen herumwindet, öffnet sich das Tal ein wenig. Überwältigt betrachtet man die Benediktinerabtei Beuron, die auf einer kleinen Anhöhe inmitten des gleichnamigen Marktfleckens liegt. Zusammen mit der nahezu unberührten Natur dieses Donauabschnitts bildet das Tal einen Ort der Ruhe und Einkehr, weshalb es nicht zu unrecht „Tal der Mönche" genannt wird. Jeder Besucher – ob Pilger zum bekannten Gnadenbild der Schmerzensmutter in der Abteikirche St. Martin oder Durchreisender nach Ulm – wird von der kontemplativen Atmosphäre des Klosters umschlossen; schnell merkt er, dass das Leben auch außerhalb der Klostermauern von den Kirchenglocken bestimmt wird.

Im Jahr 777 wurde in dem weiten Talkessel ein erstes Kloster errichtet, danach mehrmals zerstört und umgebaut. Es war seit jeher dem Schutz des heiligen Martin von Tour anem-

winds around the rocks in a wide loop, the valley opens up a bit revealing a stunning view of the Benedictine abbey of Beuron, situated on a little hillock admidst the market town of the same name. Together with the nearly pristine nature along this section of the Danube, the valley is a peaceful, contemplative place, which is why it has rightfully been called "the valley of the monks." All visitors–whether they are passing through en route to Ulm or pilgrims headed to see the St. Martin Abbey church and its miraculous image of Our Lady of Sorrows–are enveloped in the contemplative atmosphere of the cloister. It soon becomes apparent that even life outside the cloister walls is regulated by the church bells.

The first monastery was built in this deep valley in the year 777; it was destroyed and rebuilt several times. The abbey had always been commended to the protection of

▼ Der Aachtopf, Deutschlands größte Quelle, besteht nicht zu wenigen Teilen aus Donauwasser.
▼ The Aachtopf, Germany's largest spring, consists to a large extent of water from the Danube.

▲ Die Benediktinerabtei Beuron, im Tal der Mönche gelegen, bezaubert wohl jeden Besucher.
▲ Situated in the Valley of the Monks, the Benedictine Abbey of Beuron truly captivates every visitor.

pfohlen. Noch beteten in der romanisch-gotischen Kirche jedoch keine Benediktiner, sondern Augustiner-Chorstiftsherren. Nach den verheerenden Zerstörungen während des Dreißigjährigen Krieges ließen sie das Kloster wieder aufbauen, und es entstand – auch unter dem Einfluss der bis heute lebendigen Beuroner Kunstschule – der heutige barocke Bau. Nachdem das Kloster in napoleonischen Zeiten säkularisiert und Kloster wie Ländereien dem fürstlichen Haus der Hohenzollern zugeschlagen worden waren, kamen erst in der zweiten Hälfte des 19. Jahrhunderts Benediktinermönche nach Beuron, die das Kloster übernahmen und der Regel des heiligen Benedikts unterordneten.

Wer die Spiritualität des Ortes erleben möchte, der sollte die Abteikirche beispielsweise in der Zeit der Vesper besuchen und sich in einer der Kirchenbänke niederlassen. Indem man den lateinischen Gesängen der Mönche zuhört, vergisst man in der schönen Beuroner Kirche für eine kurze Weile die Welt

St. Martin of Tour, but it was no longer Benedictines praying in the Romanesque-Gothic church; they were replaced by the choral canons of Augustinians. After it was destroyed in the Thirty Years' War, they rebuilt the complex in its current baroque style, reflecting the influence of the Beuron Art School, which is still active today. After the abbey was secularized in the Napoleonic era, and monasteries as well as estates were appropriated by the royal House of Hohenzollern, Benedictine monks finally returned to Beuron in the second half of the nineteenth century. They took over the abbey and submitted to the Rule of St. Benedict.

A wonderful way to experience the spirituality of this place is to visit the abbey church during vespers and take a seat in the church pews. Listening to the monks chanting in Latin in the beautiful sanctuary of Beuron, the world around you fades away for a short while, and later you

um sich herum und kehrt anschließend ruhig und körperlich und seelisch erfrischt in diese zurück.

In ausgedehnten Mäandern schlängelt sich die Donau weiter Richtung Sigmaringen, die Felsspitzen am Ufer sind nun mit Burgen und Ruinen besetzt: Die Burgen Kallenberg und Wildenstein, die Schlösser Bronnen und Werenwag und die Ruinen von Schloss Hausen und Falkenstein überragen den noch jungen Fluss. Sie alle zeugen nicht nur von der einstigen Bedeutung der Region Obere Donau, sie sind auch Schauplätze zahlloser Legenden und schaurig-trauriger Geschichten. Unterhalb der Felsen ist der Platz rar geworden: Straße und Eisenbahn finden nur wenig Raum, dem Lauf des Flusses zu folgen – immer wieder müssen sie den Kalkfels unterqueren, „Tore" wurden zu diesem Zweck in den Stein gehauen.

Vielen gilt die Landschaft der oberen Donau als der schönste Donauabschnitt überhaupt. Der Fluss hat sich hier einen ländlichen Charme erhalten, den er so erst wieder bei Wien in den Donauauen und danach in der Dobrudscha in

▼ Die Straßen entlang der Donau sind schmal und oft von Tunneln beschattet.
▼ The streets along the Danube are narrow and frequently pass through tunnels.

rejoin it in a more peaceful state of mind, physically and mentally refreshed.

The Danube meanders in expansive loops in the direction of Sigmaringen, its jagged rocks now topped with castles and ruins. The castles of Kallenberg and Wildenstein, the palaces of Bronnen and Werenwag, and the Hausen and Falkenstein palace ruins tower over a river that is still in its early stages. All of them not only testify to the former prominence of the Upper Danube, they are also the settings for countless legends and eerily sad tales. Space has become scarce beneath the rocks; streets and trains have only a narrow margin in which to follow the course of the river and repeatedly have to travel through "gates" that have been carved in the limestone rock for this purpose.

Many people find the landscape of the Upper Danube to be the most beautiful section of all. The river has retained its rural charm here, a charm it only regains in the Danube meadows near Vienna, in the Dobrudscha in Romania and near the

▼ Kanufahren ist auf der ruhig fließenden Donau ein großer Spaß.
▼ Canoeing on the gently flowing Danube is great fun.

Rumänien und im Donaudelta annehmen wird. Doch während im Delta etwa eine geheimnisvolle Natur aus Altarmen, Auwäldern, schwimmenden Inseln und Galeriewäldern imponiert, beeindruckt an der oberen Donau die Mischung aus engem, felsigem Tal und den darin liegenden satten Wiesen. Dichte Wälder treffen auf Weiden, Erlen, Obstgärten und Felder, ab und zu steht ein winziges Dorf, eine Kapelle oder ein Bildstock am Wegesrand – eine harmonische Mischung aus Natur- und Kulturlandschaft. Hier entfaltet sich eine wunderbare Pflanzenwelt: Märzenbecher, Hexenkraut und Eisenhut, der Blau- und der Gelbstern sind zu finden. Wilde Orchideen wachsen beinahe in der Häufigkeit wie die vielen Kleearten, und auch Weißdorn ist an der oberen Donau nicht selten.

Felsenliebende Vögel, wie Kolkraben, Sperber, Uhus und vor allem Dohlen, teilen sich den Lebensraum mit wasserliebenden, mit Weißstörchen, Fischreihern etwa oder Kibitzen. Und auch, wenn sie hier eigentlich nicht beheimatet sind, sondern einst ausgewildert wurden, so fühlen sich die Gemsen in den Hängen des oberen Donautals doch sichtlich wohl.

◀ Der Naturpark Obere Donau ist eine perfekte Mischung aus Naur- und Kulturlandschaft.
◀ The Upper Danube Nature Preserve is a perfect combination of natural and manmade landscapes.

Danube delta. Whereas the Danube delta offers an impressive, mysterious natural world of oxbow lakes, riverside woods, floating islands and riparian forests, what is striking about the Upper Danube is the mixture of narrow rocky valleys and rich meadows nestled within them. Thick forests give way to meadows, alders, orchards, fields and the occasional tiny village, chapel or wayside shrine in a harmonious blend of natural and manmade landscapes. A fabulous plant world unfolds, including spring snowflakes, witchweed and wolfsbane, alpine squill and yellow star-of-Bethlehem. Wild orchids grow almost as prolifically as many types of clover, and the common hawthorn is also quite common in the Upper Danube region.

Rock-loving birds such as ravens, sparrow hawks, eagle owls and above all jackdaws share their habitat with waterfowl including white storks, herons and northern lapwings. And even though they are not actually native to the area but were released into the wild, chamois feel right at home on the slopes of the Upper Danube.

Weiter flussabwärts wird das Donautal deutlich weiter, und Sigmaringen kommt in Sicht. Die beschauliche Stadt mit ihrer hübschen Altstadt wird von dem gigantischen Hohenzollernschloss dominiert, das mit Zinnen, Türmen und Erkern ganz dem Schlossideal des Historismus verschrieben ist. Doch man findet – neben den eher kitschigen Umbauten und Accessoires des 19. Jahrhunderts – auch Originalteile aus der Stauferzeit wie den Bergfried und den Palas. Das Schloss hat eine wechsel- und nicht immer ehrenvolle Geschichte: Nicht nur Fürsten wurden hier zur Welt gebracht und haben hier gelebt, auch Teilen des französischen Vichy-Regimes – darunter Marschall Pétain selbst – bot die Gestapo hier im Zweiten Weltkrieg vor den Alliierten Unterschlupf.

Floss die Donau bislang eher Richtung Nordosten, so schlägt sie nun einen südöstlichen Kurs Richtung Ulm ein. Die Landschaft ist deutlich stärker besiedelt, Überreste einer

Further downstream the Danube Valley becomes distinctly wider and Sigmaringen comes into view. The peaceful city with its pretty old town is dominated by the gigantic Hohenzollern palace. With its battlements, towers and oriels, it is the embodiment of an ideal historicist castle. Alongside the rather kitschy nineteenth-century renovations and additions, however, there are original sections from the Staufer period, including the keep and the Great Hall. The castle has a checkered, less than honorable past. Not only princes were born and lived here; it is also the place where members of the French Vichy regime, including Marshall Pétain himself, offered the Gestapo a hideout from the Allies during World War II.

So far, the Danube has flowed in a northeasterly direction, but now it turns to the southeast in the direction of Ulm. The landscape is clearly more densely populated, and the remains of a sixth-century Celtic settlement, Heuneburg, have been

▾ Das Schloss der Hohenzollern in Sigmaringen: ein Postkartenmotiv und Paradebeispiel für den Eklektizismus
▾ The Hohenzollern Castle in Sigmaringen: a picture-perfect, classic example of Eclecticism

▲ Von Kloster Obermarchtal bietet sich ein letzter Blick über das schöne Donautal, bevor diese in die Ulmer Alb eintritt.
▲ Marchtal Abbey in Obermarchtal offers a final view over the beautiful Danube Valley before the river enters the Ulm Alb.

keltischen Siedlung aus dem 6. Jahrhundert, die Heuneburg, wurden hier ausgegraben. Das Donautal ist nun weitläufig und wird merklich flacher; Ackerbau dominiert hier. Noch aber darf die Donau in weiten Kehren fließen, überwindet nur ab und zu kleinere Staustufen und Pumpwerke. Bei der barocken, aufgelassenen Prämonstratenserabtei Obermarchtal – deren Kirche und Atmosphäre sehr erlebenswert sind – bietet sich noch einmal ein grandioser Ausblick auf die Donau, danach beginnt ganz allmählich der Einfluss Ulms zu wirken. Zunächst werden die Donauschleifen immer kleiner, dann fließt der Fluss schnurgerade und eingezwängt in ein künstliches Bett auf Ulm und Neu-Ulm zu.

In Ulm sollte der erste Weg zu dem ab 1377 errichteten Münster und der zweite auf dessen Turm hinaufführen. Der ist mit 161,6 Metern Höhe der höchste Kirchturm der Welt, und es ist ein echtes Erlebnis, ihn zu besteigen – jedenfalls für alle Schwindelfreien. Denn das lichte gotische Maßwerk des

excavated here. The Danube Valley is broader and noticeably flatter in this section, and agriculture dominates the landscape. Yet the Danube is still allowed to flow in wide loops, reined in only occasionally by smaller barrages and pumping stations. The abandoned, baroque-style Premonstratensian abbey of Obermarchtal—whose church and overall ambiance should not be missed—offers another magnificent view of the Danube. Thereafter, the influence of Ulm then gradually begins to take hold. The curves in the Danube become increasingly small until the river flows straight as an arrow, forced through an artificial riverbed into Ulm and Neu-Ulm.

In Ulm, the first order of events is to visit the minster, begun in 1377, and the second is to climb up its tower. At 161.6 meters (530 feet), it is the highest church tower in the world. Even if the tower wasn't completed until 1890, it is still an amazing experience to climb to the top, provided you aren't afraid of heights. The light tracery is covered by

erst im Jahr 1890 vollendeten Turms ist nur selten durch Gitter gesichert, der Blick schweift frei auf die baden-württembergische Landschaft links der Donau bzw. die nun bayerische Landschaft und die Stadt Neu-Ulm auf dem rechten Donauufer. Immer weiter führen die Wendeltreppen den Turm hinauf, vorbei an der Glockenstube, über zwei Aussichtsplateaus und dann noch einmal die letzten ausgetretenen Stufen herauf. Oben angekommen pfeift der Wind, und man hat auf 143 Metern einen phänomenalen Rundblick.

Im Innern des Münsters lässt sich der Ulmer Spatz bestaunen. Eine Kopie dieses ursprünglich auf dem Münster installierten Vogels ist nicht nur wieder auf dem Kirchendach, sondern auch überall in der Stadt in Pappmaschee und knalligen Farben anzutreffen. Der Sage nach brauchten die Ulmer zum Bau ihres Münsters einen besonders langen Balken, den

grating only in a few places, providing an unobstructed view of the landscape of Baden-Württemberg left of the Danube, and of the Bavarian landscape and the city of Neu-Ulm on the right bank. The spiral staircase leads ever upward beyond the bell tower, past two viewing platforms, and up the last well-worn steps. Once the pinnacle is reached, at a height of 143 meters (469 feet), the wind whistles and you are rewarded with a phenomenal panoramic view.

Inside the church, you can admire the famous sparrow of Ulm. Replicas of this bird, originally installed atop the minster, are found not only on the church roof, but all over the city in brightly colored paper maché. According to legend, the citizens of Ulm needed an especially long beam to build their minster, but they were carrying it crosswise and could not figure out how to get it through the city gate. Then

▾ Ulm (rechts) und Neu-Ulm (links) – vom Turm des Münsters aus stromaufwärts gesehen
▾ Ulm (right) and Neu-Ulm (left), as seen looking upstream from the tower of the Ulm Minster

▲ Wer die letzten Stufen des Turms erklimmt, wird mit einem wunderbaren Ausblick und dem Wissen belohnt, dass er auf dem höchsten Kirchturm der Welt steht.
▲ Anyone who makes it up the very last steps to the tower is rewarded by a wonderful, panoramic view and can be proud to stand at the top of the world's highest church tower.

▲ Das idyllische Fischerviertel – von der Blau durchflossen – ist neben dem Ulmer Münster die zweite Touristenattraktion.
▲ The second most popular tourist attraction in Ulm, after the minster, is the idyllic Fishermens Quarter – with the Blau flowing right through it.

sie aber – weil sie ihn quer trugen – partout nicht durchs Stadttor bringen konnten. Da beobachteten sie einen Spatzen beim Nestbau, der einen Ast, um ihn durch eine schmale Stelle zu bringen, längs im Schnabel trug. Die Ulmer versuchten dasselbe mit dem Balken. Seitdem gemahnt der Spatz die Ulmer jeden Tag daran, dass es sich lohnt, manchmal umzudenken und andere Wege zu beschreiten.

Der Weg vom Münster zum Donauufer führt durch das reizende Fischerviertel. Seine Fachwerkhäuser werden von der Blau durchflossen, die im Blautopf – der strahlend blau erscheinenden Karstquelle bei Blaubeuren – entspringt und in Ulm in die Donau mündet. In den Blautopf soll einst ein Donaunix vom Schwarzen Meer seine Frau, die schöne Lau, verbannt haben, weil diese nicht lachen konnte. Nachdem sie dies endlich gelernt hatte, durfte sie über Ulm in die Donau zurückkehren. In dem alten Fischer- und Gerberviertel der Stadt, in dem sich heute Touristen wie Einheimische am Abend an schwäbischen Spezialitäten und Gold-Ochsen-Bier

they observed a sparrow carrying a branch lengthwise in its beak in order to fit it through a small space. The Ulmers tried the same thing with the beam, and ever since then, the sparrow reminds the people of Ulm every day that is often worthwhile to rethink things and take a different path.

The route from the minster to the bank of the Danube leads through the charming fisherman's quarter. The Blau River runs by its half-timbered houses and has it source in the Blau Spring, which flows into the Danube at Ulm. The spring appears bright blue at its source in the karst near the town of Blaubeuren. Once upon a time, a Danube water sprite from the Black Sea supposedly exiled his wife, the beautiful Lau, to the Blue Spring because she could not laugh. When she finally learned how, she was allowed to return to the Danube via Ulm. In the old fishermens' and tanners' quarters of the city, tourists and locals alike enjoy Swabian specialties and Gold-Ochsen beer. At one time, the people lived from and with these two rivers. The fishermen pulled pike, zander

▲ Das Ulmer Umland wird landwirtschaftlich intensiv genutzt.
▲ The land surrounding Ulm is used extensively for farming.

▲ Dennoch findet die Pflanzenwelt immer wieder ein Fleckchen, sich zu entfalten.
▲ And still the fauna always finds a niche where it can unfold.

laben, lebten die Menschen einst von und mit den beiden Flüssen. Die Fischer zogen aus der Donau Hechte, Zander und Barsche, und von hier aus starteten die berühmten Ulmer Schachteln ihre Fahrten flussabwärts. Die Einwegboote, die ursprünglich aus Wien stammten und dort Zillen heißen, ersetzten bereits ab dem 17. Jahrhundert Flöße, um Waren oder Personen flussabwärts zu transportieren – sogar bis ins Donaudelta. An ihrem Bestimmungsort wurden die schwarzweiß gestreiften Boote zerlegt und das Holz weiterverkauft.

Außer mit den Schachteln, die wenig Tiefgang haben, ist die Schifffahrt auf der Donau auch hinter Ulm noch nicht möglich. Dennoch ist es mit der Donauidylle hinter Ulm für einige Kilometer vorbei – Industrie, ein Kernkraftwerk, intensiver Ackerbau und ein noch immer schnurgerader Fluss bestimmen die Gegend. Noch einmal entfalten sich zwar Auwälder und ein Niedermoor mit einer eigenen, noch intakten Flora und Fauna im sogenannten Schwäbischen Donaumoos hinter Günzburg, und Neuburg an der Donau lockt mit einem

(perch) and bass from the Danube, and it was from here that the famous *Ulmer schachtel*, a special kind of barge, began their journeys downriver. The one-way boats originally came from Vienna, where they were called *zillen*. From the seventeenth century onward they replaced rafts, and were used to transport goods and people downriver to points as far away as the Danube delta. The black-and-white striped boats were dismantled at their destinations, and the wood was resold.

Even after Ulm, boat travel on the Danube is not yet possible except by *schachtel*, which have a shallow draft. All the same, the Danube is far from idyllic for a few miles beyond Ulm: industry, a nuclear power plant, intensive agriculture and an utterly straight river course determine the landscape. Admittedly, just past Günzburg woods fan out again alongside the river and there is a low moor with a unique and still intact flora and fauna, known as the Swabian Danube Moor. Neuburg an der Donau also entices visitors with its captivating Renaissance palace. Near the Bavarian garrison city of Ingol-

bezaubernden Renaissanceschloss, doch bei der bayerischen Garnisonsstadt Ingolstadt wirkt die Donaulandschaft wieder urban. Industrie, vor allem Automobil- und Ölindustrie, hat sich rund um die Stadt niedergelassen. Und Ingolstadt ist die Stadt der Bieres: Denn 1516 wurde in ihr das bayerische Reinheitsgebot, das dem deutschen Reinheitsgebot als Vorlage diente, erlassen. Doch vor allem ist Ingolstadt für seine Soldaten bekannt.

Bereits in der Jungsteinzeit besiedelt, errichteten die Römer am Ort des heutigen Ingolstadt ein Kastell zur Sicherung des Limes. Und dort, wo bereits römische Legionäre Brücken über den Fluss schlugen, hat sich die Militärtradition über Jahrhunderte hinweg erhalten. Im 19. und 20. Jahrhundert war Ingolstadt Garnisonsstadt, in der weit mehr als die Hälfte der Einwohner Soldaten waren, und heute lernen die Pioniere der Bundeswehr hier, Pontonbrücken über die Donau zu bauen.

stadt, however, the Danube landscape again takes on an urban appearance. Industry, particularly oil and automobile, has established itself around the city. And Ingolstadt is a city of breweries; the Bavarian Beer Purity Law was enacted here in 1516, 1516, the law that served as the model for the influential and long-lived German Beer Purity Law *(Reinheitsgebot)*. But first and foremost, Ingolstadt is known for its soldiers.

This area was first settled way back in the Neolithic Age, and the Romans built a fortress where present-day Ingolstadt now stands to secure the border. In the place where Roman legions once built bridges across the river, military tradition has been preserved over many centuries. In the nineteenth and twentieth centuries, Ingolstadt was a garrison city in which well over half of the residents were soldiers, and today German army engineers learn to build pontoon bridges spanning the Danube.

▼ Der Festungsturm Triva in Ingolstadt
▼ Triva Tower, part of the fortress in Ingolstadt

Es dauert nur wenige Flusskilometer und die Donaulandschaft verändert sich wieder grundlegend. Die Äcker zur Linken hinter sich lassend, schmiegt sich der Naturpark Altmühltal an den Fluss, und die Donau muss sich wiederum durch hohes Kalkgestein winden. Diesen Donaudurchbruch genannten Abschnitt, auf dem die Donau die Fränkische Alb, aber auch einen Teil des bayerischen Hopfenanbaugebietes Holledau durchquert, durchfährt man am besten mit dem Boot. In engen Kehren schlängelt sich die Donau durch die dicht bewaldeten Kalkfelsen, die Strömung nimmt sichtlich zu, und wenn sich der enge Durchbruch an einer Kurve auf der rechten Seite etwas öffnet, wird man von der traumhaften Benediktinerabtei Weltenburg überrascht. Auch architektonisch perfekt der Donauschleife angepasst, ist das Kloster mit seinem im Sommer herrlichen Biergarten ein Ziel für fromme Pilger ebenso wie für sonntägliche Kirchgänger, Wanderer im Altmühltal, Radwanderer entlang des Donauradwegs oder die Liebhaber von Klosterwurst, -käse und natürlich dem hausei-

Just a short way downriver, the Danube landscape changes dramatically. Leaving behind the farmland to the left of the river, the Altmühl Valley Nature Preserve nestles up to the riverbank and once again, the Danube has to wind its way through high limestone rock formations. This section, called the Danube Gorge, is where the Danube crosses the Franconian Alb and part of Bavaria's Holledau, the largest area of hop cultivation in the world, and it is best traveled by boat. As the Danube winds it way through the thickly forested limestone rocks in a series of tight bends, the current becomes visibly stronger. And when the narrow Danube Gorge opens up slightly on the right side at a bend in the river, there stands a welcome surprise, the enchanting Benedictine Abbey of Weltenburg. The monastery's architecture harmonizes perfectly with the river bend, and the abbey's wonderful beer garden is a favorite summer destination for devout pilgrims, Sunday churchgoers, people hiking in the Altmühl Valley or biking along the Danube bike path. The abbey's special sausage,

▼ Die Abtei Weltenburg am Beginn des Donaudurchbruchs wird nicht nur wegen ihrer barocken Pracht, sondern auch wegen des Klosterlikörs und des Biergartens geschätzt.
▼ Weltenburg Abbey at the head of the Danube Gorge is revered not only for its baroque splendor, but also for its beer and beer garden.

▲ Obwohl in weiten Teilen künstlich angelegt, hat auch der Main-Donau-Kanal seine Idyllen zu bieten – wie hier Schloss Prunn.
▲ Although large sections of it are manmade, the Main-Danube Canal still has its own charm, as here at Schloss Prunn.

genen Weltenburger Bitter und Bier. Das Herzstück des Klosters aber ist seine prachtvolle barocke Abteikirche: Die an der Stelle eines keltischen Opferplatzes bzw. später eines römischen Tempels zu Ehren von Minerva und Apollo errichtete Kirche wurde zwischen 1716 und 1739 von den Gebrüdern Cosmas Damian und Egid Quirin Asam komplett im Stil des Spätbarocks umgebaut und mit farbenprächtigen Fresken, herrlichen Stukkaturen und einem beeindruckenden Altar zu Ehren des heiligen Georgs, des Schutzpatrons der Kirche, ausgestaltet.

Überquert man das Altmühltal Richtung Nordwesten, so trifft man bald auf den Main-Donau-Kanal, der den Main in Bamberg mit der Donau in Kelheim verbindet und es letztendlich ermöglicht, dass Europa per Schiff von Rotterdam bis Constanta am Schwarzen Meer durchquert werden könnte. Einen ersten Kanal weihte König Ludwig I. von Bayern 1846 ein, weshalb dieser noch heute Ludwigskanal genannt wird; der neue

cheese and, of course, its own Weltenburg bitters and beer brewed on site also draw their share of fans. But the heart ofthe monastery is its magnificent baroque church. The abbey church is located on the spot of a former Celtic sacrificial site and a subsequent Roman temple in honor of Minerva and Apollo. Between 1716 and 1739, it was completely renovated in the late baroque style by the Asam brothers, Cosmas Damian and Egid Quirin, and decorated with colorful frescoes, magnificent stuccowork and an impressive altar dedicated to St. George, the church's patron saint.

Crossing the Altmühl Valley in a northwesterly direction, one soon reaches the Main-Danube Canal, that connects the Main River in Bamberg with the Danube in Kelheim, finally making it possible to cross Europe by ship from Rotterdam to Constanta on the Black Sea. King Ludwig I of Bavaria dedicated the first canal here in 1846, which is why it is still called the *Ludwigskanal* today. The new canal

Kanal wurde 1992 fertiggestellt und heißt nun Rhein-Main-Donau-Kanal. Die Landschaft am Unterlauf des Kanals führt ebenfalls durch das idyllische Altmühltal und übt mit ihren burgenbekrönten, bewaldeten Hängen einen ganz eigenen Charme aus.

Kurz bevor Donau und Kanal die Stadt Kelheim erreichen und dort zusammenfließen, thront auf den Felsen des Durchbruchs weithin sichtbar auf dem Michelsberg die mächtige Befreiungshalle. Der Zentralbau im Stil der römischen Antike wurde zwischen 1842 und 1863 unter König Ludwig I. von Bayern im Gedenken an die Befreiungskriege errichtet. Nachdem der Russlandfeldzug Napoleons scheiterte, kam es auch in den deutschen Ländern zum Befreiungskampf gegen Napoleon. Die Koalition der Napoleongegner konnte mit der Völkerschlacht bei Leipzig im Oktober 1813 erste Siege für sich verbuchen und zwang den französischen Herrscher durch die Einnahme von Paris im März 1814 zur Abdankung. Knapp 30

was completed in 1992 and is called the Rhine-Main-Danube Canal. The landscape on its lower course also passes through the idyllic Altmühl Valley, where the forested slopes crowned with castles have a unique charm.

Shortly before the Danube and the canal come together in the city of Kelheim, the monumental *Befreiungshalle* ("Hall of Liberation") crowns the rocks of the Danube Gorge and is visible for miles around from its perch on Mount Michelsberg. Built between 1842 and 1863 under King Ludwig I of Bavaria, the central-plan building in the style of Roman antiquity is a monument to the Wars of Liberation. After the failure of Napoleon's Russian campaign, a fight for independence from Napoleon ensued on German soil. The coalition against Napoleon was able to record its first victory in October 1813 at the Battle of Nations near Leipzig. By taking Paris in March 1814, the coalition also forced the French sovereign to abdicate. Just thirty years later, King

◄ Im Winter entfaltet der Donaudurchbruch bei Kelheim seinen ganzen Zauber.
◄ The Danube Gorge near Kelheim exerts a special magic in wintertime.
▼ Weithin sichtbar: die Befreiungshalle bei Kelheim
▼ Visible from afar: the *Befreiungshalle* ("Hall of Liberation") near Kelheim

▲ König Ludwig I. von Bayern ließ die Halle im Andenken an die Befreiungskriege gegen Napoleon errichten.
▲ King Ludwig I of Bavaria had the Hall of Liberation built as a memorial to the Wars of Liberation against Napoleon.

Jahre später ehrte Ludwig I. bei Kelheim mit dem nach antikem Vorbild errichteten, monumentalen Zentralbau die tapferen Befreiungskrieger. „Ewig währet euer Thaten Glanz", dichtete der König zum Anlass der Grundsteinlegung. Das Äußere zieren 18 Kolossalstatuen als Allegorien der deutschen Volksstämme und Symbol für deren Einigung nach den Befreiungskriegen. Im Innern halten Siegesgöttinnen aus weißem Carrara-Marmor vergoldete Schilde. Sie wurden aus der Bronze der siegreichen Geschütze gegossen.

Am Ausgang des Donaudurchbruchs kann sich der Fluss nun wieder behaglich ausbreiten, zumal er in Kelheim am Zusammenfluss von Donau und Main-Donau-Kanal noch einmal deutlich breiter wird. Nachdem die Donau die Wälder des Altmühltals hinter sich gelassen hat, tritt sie nun vor Regensburg in eine von Ackerbau geprägte, flache Landschaft ein, die linker Hand vom Bayerischen Wald begrenzt wird.

Ludwig commissioned the Befreiungshalle to be built in honor of the brave freedom fighters. "May your shining deeds last forever," the king wrote on the occasion of the laying of the cornerstone. Eighteen colossal statues adorn the exterior as an allegory for the German tribes and as a symbol of their unification following the Wars of Liberation. Inside, the gods of victory are carved of white Carrara marble and carry gold-plated shields that were poured from the bronze of the victorious guns.

At the end of the Danube Gorge, the river can spread out in its bed comfortably, especially since it becomes noticeably wider at the confluence of the Danube and the Main-Danube Canal in Kelheim. After the Danube has left behind the forests of the Altmühl Valley, but before it reaches Regensburg, the river enters a flat landscape dominated by agriculture. The Bavarian Forest borders it on the left-hand side.

Als viertgrößte Stadt in Bayern ist Regensburg nicht nur touristisch, sondern auch wirtschaftlich von Bedeutung. Die ansonsten eher dünn besiedelte Oberpfalz ist bereits ab Kelheim deutlich belebter, und rund um Regensburg zeigt sich das typische Bild einer von Gewerbe- und Industrieparks dominierten Großstadt. Dazu bildet die Altstadt von Regensburg einen wunderbaren Kontrast. Die zentralen Bauten des einstigen römischen Legionslagers Castra Regina sind der alles beherrschende Dom St. Peter und die Steinerne Brücke, berühmt aber auch die Altstadt selbst, das Residenzschloss derer zu Thurn und Taxis, St. Emmeram, und – vor den Toren der Stadt – die Walhalla. Der Dom, ab 1260 errichtet, gilt als eines der bedeutendsten Werke der Gotik in Bayern. Weltweit ist er aber vor allem durch seinen Domchor, die Regensburger Domspatzen, bekannt, einen der ältesten und berühmtesten Knabenchöre der Welt. Für die Donaustadt von großer Bedeutung ist die Steinerne Brücke: Sie wurde zwischen 1135

As the fourth largest city in Bavaria, Regensburg is important not only as a tourist destination, but also as an economic center. From Kelheim onward, the otherwise sparsely populated Upper Palatinate is clearly more lively, and around Regensburg it has the typical look of a large city dominated by business and industrial parks. The old town section of Regensburg provides a wonderful counterpoint. The central structures of the erstwhile Roman legionary fortress Castra Regina are the all-dominating St. Peter's Cathedral and the Stone Bridge. The old town is also famous in its own right, including St. Emmeran Castle, for example, the residence of the Princely House of Thurn and Taxis; and Walhalla stands just outside the city gates. St. Peter's Cathedral was begun in 1260, and is recognized as one of the most important Gothic works in Bavaria, but it is chiefly known for its cathedral choir, the Regensburger Domspatzen, one of the oldest and most renowned boys choirs in the world. The Stone Bridge is the oldest stationary bridge spanning a

▾ Mit der berühmten Steinernen Brücke und dem Dom St. Peter gehört die Altstadt von Regensburg zum UNESCO-Weltkulturerbe.
▾ With its famous Stone Bridge and St. Peter's Cathedral, the old town area of Regensburg is a UNESCO World Heritage Site.

▲ „Gleichheit besteht in der Walhalla", der Ruhmeshalle der Deutschen. Kein Stand und auch nicht das weibliche Geschlecht sollen davon ausgeschlossen sein, verfügte Ludwig I.
▲ "Equality reigns in the Walhalla," the hall of fame for German speaking people. No class and not even women were to be excluded, declared Ludwig I.
◄ Mit seinen Inseln, Wasserarmen, den schönen Häusern und unvergleichlich viel Grün gleicht Regensburg einer mediterranen Kleinstadt.
◄ With its islands, tributaries, lovely houses and an incomparable quantity of greenery, Regensburg has the charm of a small Mediterranean town.

und 1146 aus Grünsandstein errichtet – für das Mittelalter eine Rekordzeit –, ist 308,71 Meter lang und besteht aus 16 steinernen Bögen, von denen heute noch 15 sichtbar sind. Sie gilt als die älteste feste Brücke über einen Fluss in Europa, wurde im Mittelalter das achte Weltwunder genannt und war Vorbild für zahllose Steinbrücken in Europa. Dass die Altstadt von Regensburg – die von vielen Wasserarmen durchzogen ist und sich auf einzelnen Inseln in der Donau ausbreitet – das am besten erhaltene Ensemble einer mittelalterlichen Groß- und Handelsstadt in Deutschland ist, hat ihr den UNESCO-Welterbestatus eingebracht.

Etwa 10 Kilometer flussabwärts überragt in einer weiten Flusskehre die Walhalla das Donautal: Die nach dem griechischen Tempelschema zwischen 1830 und 1842 errichtete

European river and is of great importance to this city on the Danube. The medieval bridge, made of green sandstone, was built between 1135 and 1146, record time by contemporary standards. It is 308.71 meters (1,013 feet) long and consists of sixteen stone arches, fifteen of which are still visible today. During the Middle Ages it was called the Eighth Wonder of the World, and it has served as the model for countless stone bridges in Europe. The old town area of Regensburg is traversed by many waterways and spreads over islands in the Donau. As the best-preserved ensemble of a large, medieval trade city in Germany, it has been accorded UNESCO World Heritage status.

Approximately 10 kilometers (6.2 miles) downstream, in a wide river bend, the Walhalla towers over the Danube Valley. Conceived along the lines of a classical Greek temple,

▲ Blick von den Stufen der Walhalla aus auf die Donau
▲ The view of the Danube from the steps of the Walhalla

Ruhmes- und Ehrenhalle wurde auf Initiative König Ludwigs I. von Bayern errichtet, der auch für die Befreiungshalle bei Kelheim verantwortlich zeichnet. Traumatisiert von seiner Kindheit unter dem „Joch" der napoleonischen Herrschaft, wollte er den Sinn der deutschen Völker für ihre gemeinsame Kultur und Geschichte stärken. Bislang wurden 128 Marmorbüsten und 64 Tafeln von Persönlichkeiten, die sich um die deutsche Kultur und Geschichte verdient gemacht haben, in der „Totenhalle" ausgestellt – darunter Büsten von Albrecht Dürer, Gotthold Ephraim Lessing, Albert Einstein und Sophie Scholl. Dass dabei schon zu Ludwigs Zeiten „kein Stand ..., auch das weibliche Geschlecht nicht" ausgeschlossen werden sollte, ist wohl dennoch der Französischen Revolution und dem Usurpator Napoleon zu verdanken. „Gleichheit besteht in der Walhalla; hebt doch der Tod jeden irdischen Unterschied auf." – Ein egalitärer Gedanke, der zu Ludwigs Zeiten im Deutschland des 19. Jahrhunderts noch nicht allzu weit verbreitet war.

Mittlerweile ist die Donau vom Oberpfälzer in den Bayerischen Wald gewechselt, der sich nordöstlich von Regensburg

the pantheon and hall of honor was built between 1830 and 1842 on the initiative of King Ludwig I of Bavaria, who was also responsible for the Hall of Liberation. Following a traumatic childhood under the "yoke" of Napoleonic rule, he wanted to strengthen the German-speaking peoples' sense of common cultural and historical roots. In the meantime, 128 marble busts and 64 tablets in the "Hall of the Dead" feature those who have earned a prominent place in Germanic history, among them Albrecht Dürer, Maria Theresa, Gotthold Ephraim Lessing, Albert Einstein, Edith Stein and Sophie Scholl. But the French Revolution and its usurper, Napoleon, are to thank for the fact that even in Ludwig's time, "no class..., not even the female sex" could be excluded. "Equality reigns in the Walhalla, for death abolishes all earthly differences" – an egalitarian thought that was not yet all that widespread in Ludwig's nineteenth-century Germany.

In the meantime, the Danube has passed from the Upper Palatinate to the Bavarian Forest, which stretches in a northeasterly

bis zur tschechischen Grenze erstreckt. In dem seltenen Naturraum wird die Donau später auf Reste von Auwäldern und einige Altarme treffen. Dichte Mischwälder werden sich manchmal an ihre Hänge schmiegen. Doch zunächst geht es weiter durch fruchtbares Ackerland, und nur im Hinterland zeigt der Naturpark Bayerischer Wald mit seinen Bannwäldern vielerorts noch sein natürliches Gesicht.

Die Donau selbst hat mit dem Einfließen des Rhein-Main-Donau-Kanals, vor allem aber hinter Regensburg ihr Antlitz geändert: ein breiter Strom, der zwar immer noch in weiten, doch merklich begradigten Bögen durch Deutschland fließt, von Staustufen durchsetzt ist und dessen Ufer nur noch erahnen lassen, dass hier einmal Altarme und Auwälder die Landschaft prägten. Stattdessen sind Lastschiffe und Schubverbände auf der Donau allgegenwärtig.

Straubing kommt ins Blickfeld, dessen Gebiet seit der Jungsteinzeit besiedelt ist, das aber vor allem durch seine mittelalterlichen Bauten auffällt. Und durch eine tragische Hinrich-

direction from Regensburg to the border of the Czech Republic. Later on, the Danube will pass the remnants of riverside woods and several oxbow lakes in the few remaining natural areas, and dense mixed forests sometimes hug its shores. But first the river flows on through fertile agricultural fields for a while, and only in its most remote corners does the Bavarian Forest Nature Preserve with its myriad protected forests show its natural face.

The Danube itself has taken on a different countenance since it was joined by the Rhein-Main-Danube Canal, particularly beyond Regensburg. It has become a broad river that still flows through Germany in wide arcs, yet they are noticeably straightened. It is interspersed with barrages, and the riverbanks only barely suggest that the landscape was once dotted with oxbow lakes and woods alongside the river. In their place, freighters and barge trains are a constant presence along the Danube.

Straubing comes into view, an area that has been inhabited since the Neolithic Age, but garners attention primarily for its medieval buildings, and for the tragic execution of

▲ Der Bayerische Wald – hier gehen Natur- und Kulturlandschaft eine perfekte Verbindung ein.
▲ The Bavarian Forest, where natural and manmade landscapes complement each other perfectly.

tung: die der Agnes Bernauer. Die war die Tochter eines Augsburger Baders und fiel eines Tages dem bayerischen Herzogssohn Albrecht ins Auge, dessen Geliebte und wahrscheinlich sogar Ehefrau sie wurde. Doch Albrechts Vater, Herzog Ernst von Bayern-München, wollte diese unstandesgemäße Mesalliance nicht hinnehmen und ließ Agnes, während sein Sohn auf der Jagd weilte, 1435 verhaften und wegen angeblicher Hexerei in die Straubinger Donau werfen. Zwar war Agnes – weil sie ertrank und Hexen ja bekanntlich oben schwimmen – rehabilitiert, doch der Herzog die unliebsame Schwiegertochter trotzdem los. Ein Jahr später ließ der Herzog auf einem Straubinger Friedhof eine Agnes-Bernauer-Kapelle errichten, die auch ein Reliefbild der Bernauerin zeigt. Sein Sohn Albrecht, der später als Herzog Albrecht III. den Beinamen der Fromme tragen sollte, ließ Agnes zu Ehren Messen lesen, heiratete aber noch im selben Jahr Anna von Braunschweig-Grubenhagen. An der Grabkapelle sollte man nicht vorbeigehen, ebenso wenig wie an der Agnes-Bernauer-Torte,

Agnes Bernauer. The daughter of an Augsburg barber, one day Agnes caught the eye of Albrecht, the son of a Bavarian duke. She became his beloved and probably also his wife. But Albrecht's father, Duke Ernst von Bayern-München, did not want to accept this unbefitting misalliance. In 1435, while his son was off hunting, he had Agnes arrested for allegedly practicing witchcraft and thrown into the Danube at Straubing. Because she drowned—and it was common knowledge that witches floated on water—Agnes was actually rehabilitated. Even so, the duke had gotten rid of his unwelcome daughter-in-law. One year later, the duke had the Agnes Bernauer Chapel built in a cemetery in Straubing, and a relief image of Agnes is displayed there. His son Albrecht would later become Duke Albrecht III, nicknamed "The Pious." He had masses said in Agnes' honor, but at the same time was married to Anna von Braunschweig-Grubenhagen within the year. Visitors should not miss the funeral chapel or a slice of Agnes Bernauer torte, a rich

einer Torte aus Nussbaiserböden mit einer Mokkabuttercreme, die im Kaffeehaus Krönner im Gedenken an die arme Baderstochter serviert wird.

Wenn die Donau die Insel Wörth (nicht zu verwechseln mit dem Ort Wörth, dessen trutziges Schloss noch vor Straubing über dem Fluss aufragt) erreicht, scheint wieder etwas Hoffnung für ihre Landschaft zu bestehen. Bald kommt man ins schöne Deggendorf mit seinen Barockkirchen, und kurz darauf mündet die Isar – im Tiroler Karwendel entspringend und über München kommend – in die Donau. In dem Mündungsgebiet kann man sich für eine kurze Weile noch einmal vorstellen, wie es an der Donau inmitten des Bayerischen Waldes vor ein paar Hundert Jahren noch ausgesehen hat. Bayerischer Amazonas wird das Gebiet von den stolzen Bajuvaren gern genannt, und auch wenn das Naturschutzgebiet nicht annähernd die Größe Amazoniens erreicht, kann man den Vergleich durchaus nachvollziehen. Die Auwälder, Sumpfwiesen, Röhrichte und Altwässer sind der Lebensraum unzähliger

cake with mocha buttercream on a nut meringue base, which is served at the Krönner Café in memory of the poor duchess.

When the Danube reaches the Island of Wörth (not to be confused with the city of Wörth, whose defiant castle looms over the river well before Straubing) the landscape seems to become more promising again. Not far downriver is the beautiful town of Deggendorf with its baroque churches, and shortly thereafter the Isar flows into the Danube. The Isar River has its source in the Karwendel Mountains in the Tyrol and flows to the Danube via Munich. In the area where the two rivers meet, it is still possible to imagine what it might have looked like alongside the Danube in the middle of the Bavarian Forest several hundred years ago. Proud, old-time Bavarians like to call it the "Bavarian Amazon," and even if the nature preserve doesn't come close to the Amazon Rainforest in size, one can certainly understand how the comparison came about. The forests alongside the river, marshy meadows, reed beds and shallow oxbow lakes provide the habitat for

▼ Auf bayerischen Barock trifft man an der Donau allenthalben – hier in Deggendorf.
▼ Examples of Bavarian baroque architecture are ubiquitous along the Danube, as here in Deggendorf.

▼ In den Auwäldern des „bayrischen Amazonas"
▼ In the riverside forests of the "Bavarian Amazon"

▲ Das Blaukehlchen ist wohl einer der hübschesten Bewohner des Isarmündungsgebietes.
▲ The bluethroat is surely one of the prettiest inhabitants of the Isar estuary.

vom Aussterben bedrohter geschützter und schützenswerter Tier- und Pflanzenarten.

Sumpfgladiole, Teufelskralle und Hauswurz wachsen auf den Wiesen, Blaukehlchen, Eisvogel, Halsbandschnäpper und Pirol singen in Schilf und Wald, der Moorfrosch laicht in den Altwässern, und im Wasser tummeln sich Fische, von deren Namen man nur selten hört, wie zum Beispiel Huchen, Rapfen oder Schrätzer. Und es gibt wenige Orte in Deutschland, an denen man noch den Silbergrünen Bläuling (ein Tagfalter), die Vogel-Azurjungfer und die Blaugrüne Mosaikjungfer (beides Libellenarten) oder das Nachtpfauenauge beobachten kann. Auf dem Grund zwischen Deggendorf und Isarmündungsgebiet werden zudem seit dem Jahr 2004 wieder Auerochsen, auch Ur genannt, rückgezüchtet, die man auf einer eingezäunten Weide beobachten kann.

countless protected and endangered species of plants and animals, as well as those that are at least worthy of protection.

Marsh gladiolus, devil's claw and the common houseleek (hen and chicks) grow in the meadows. Bluethroats, kingfishers, collared flycatchers and orioles sing among the reeds and in the forest. Moor frogs spawn in the shallow oxbow lakes, and fish of species rarely encountered–such as Danube salmon, asps, and schraetzer–inhabit the water. And there are few places in Germany where it is still possible to see Chalkhill blues (a type of butterfly), ornate bluets and southern hawkers (two species of dragonflies), and saturnia moths. On the land between Deggendorf and the Isar estuary, since 2004 a special type of cattle, the auroch, an ancestor of domestic cattle, can be observed in a fenced-in meadow. Also called urus, they have been selectively bred back into existence.

Die Donau verlässt dieses Paradies etwa bei der Stadt Niederalteich. Deren Benediktinerkloster, Niederaltaich geschrieben, ist eines der wenigen Klöster Deutschlands, in dem die Mönche zwei liturgische Traditionen pflegen, nämlich die römische und die byzantinische. So kann das Kloster sowohl eine gotische, barockisierte Hallenkirche, in der der römische Ritus vollzogen wird, sein Eigen nennen, als auch eine byzantinische Kirche. Es ist ein einmaliges und recht ungewohntes Erlebnis, an dem Gebet der Mönche, die nach byzantinischem Ritus leben, teilzunehmen. Auch wenn das eigentliche Geschehen hinter der Ikonostase stattfindet, sind allein die A-capella-Gesänge und die für Deutschland fremdartige Kirchenausstattung beeindruckend. Dass man in der angeschlossenen Gaststätte Klosterhof Niederaltaich auch eine anständige Brotzeit und die Altaicher Klosterbitter – im

The Danube departs this paradise somewhere near the village of Niederalteich. Its Benedictine abbey, spelled Niederaltaich, is one of the very few monasteries in Germany where the monks observe two liturgical traditions, namely the Roman and the Byzantine. The abbey thus has both a Byzantine church and a Gothic-turned-baroque hall church, in which the Roman rite is used. It is a unique and unusual experience to share in the prayers of the monks who live according to the Byzantine rite. Even if the actual events take place behind the iconostasis (a screen diving the sanctuary from the nave in Eastern Orthodox churches) the a cappella singing and—by German standards—exotic ecclesiastical setting are impressivein themselves. You can get a very respectable bite to eat and Altaich Cloister bitters at the restaurant in the adjoining monastery courtyard—in the summer months, of

▼ In den Auwäldern der Isarmündung darf sich der Fluss frei entfalten, sodass auch bedrohte Insekten-, Schnecken- und Muschelarten einen geschützten Lebensraum finden.
▼ In the wooded areas of the Isar estuary, the river can develop unhindered, so that even endangered insects, snails and mussels find a protected habitat.

▲ Farbige Häuser säumen die Ufer in der Dreiflüssestadt Passau.
▲ Colorful houses line the banks of Passau, the city on three rivers.

Sommer natürlich im Biergarten – bekommt, rundet den Besuch der Benediktinerabtei perfekt ab.

In nunmehr wieder weiten Mäandern nimmt die Donau ihren Lauf, passiert zahlreiche Inseln (zum Beispiel einmal mehr: Wörth) und erreicht schließlich Passau, das bereits an der deutsch-österreichischen Grenze liegt. Mit dem Stephansdom, der Alten Residenz, Opern- und Rathaus, dem ehemaligen Benediktinerkloster Niedernburg, den Vesten Oberhaus und Niederhaus und den farbenfrohen Häusern der Altstadt reiht sich eine Sehenswürdigkeit an die andere. Vor allem den etwas beschwerlichen Weg hinauf zur Veste Oberhaus – ab 1219 errichtet und stetig um- und ausgebaut – sollte man unbedingt auf sich nehmen. Von der ehemaligen Burg und Residenz des fürstlichen Bischofs von Passau aus lässt sich nämlich das interessanteste Phänomen der Stadt betrachten: der

course, in the beer garden. What a perfect way to round off a visit to the Benedictine abbey.

The Danube continues on its way, meandering in wide arcs, passing numerous islands (including Wörth for a second time) and finally reaching Passau, located on the German-Austrian border. One impressive sight follows another: the Stephansdom (St. Steven's Cathedral), the Old Residence, the opera house and city hall, the former Benedictine abbey of Niedernburg, the Oberhaus and Niederhaus fortifications, and the colorful houses of the old town. The path up to the Veste Oberhaus (Oberhaus fortification) is rather arduous, but is absolutely worthwhile. Begun in 1219, and it has been renovated and expanded ever since. The former fortress and residence of the prince-bishops of Passau provides the perfect vantage point to observe the most interesting phenomenon the

Zusammenfluss von Ilz, Inn und Donau. Es ist ein ganz eigenes Naturschauspiel, das sich nach dem Aufstieg bietet und das so nur von hier oder aus der Luft erkennbar wird: In drei unterschiedlichen Farben fließen die Flüsse zusammen. Von links kommend mündet direkt unterhalb der Veste die schwarz-braune Ilz aus den Moorlandschaften des Bayerischen Waldes in die Donau. Aus ihr wurden einst wertvolle schwarze Süßwasserflussperlen, die sogenannten Passauer Perlen, für den Bischof gefischt. Wer beim „Schwarzfischen" erwischt wurde, dem ließ der Bischof die Hände abhacken.

Wenige Meter flussabwärts trifft die Donau in ihrem schlammigen Braun auf den milchig-grünen Inn – der hier wesentlich mächtiger ist als die Donau und daher für eine Weile noch die Farbe derselben bestimmt. Wir verlassen die Dreiflüssestadt, die bald danach für die kommenden knapp dreißig Flusskilometer schon Grenzfluss zwischen Deutsch-

city has to offer: the confluence of the Ilz, the Inn and the Danube. This unique natural drama unfolds only after making the climb, for it is only visible from this spot or from the air: the three rivers flowing together have distinct colors. Directly below the fortress, the black-brown Ilz emerges from the marshlands of the Bavarian Forest and flows into the Danube from the left. At one time, valuable, black freshwater pearls, also called "Passau pearls," were harvested from the Ilz River for the bishops. Anyone who was caught "fishing on the black market" had his hands cut off by order of the bishop.

A short distance downstream, the muddy-brown Danube meets the milky green Inn, which is substantially more powerful than the Danube at this point, and therefore determines the color of the water for a ways. We are now leaving the city on three rivers, and shortly the Danube will be the border between Germany and Austria for the next 30 kilo-

▾ Von der Veste Oberhaus lässt sich das Farbspiel am Zusammenfluss von schwarzer Ilz (ganz vorn), Donau (Mitte) und grünem Inn (hinten) gut betrachten.
▾ The Oberhaus fortification is a good vantage point from which to observe the confluence of the black Ilz (foreground), the Danube (middle) and the "green" Inn (background).

▲ Die bezaubernde Nixe Isa, die an den Gestaden der Donau der Legende nach Schiffsleute bezirzte, betört heutzutage auch Radler und andere Ausflügler.
▲ The mesmerizing mermaid Isa: according to legend, she bewitched shipmen from the shores of the Danube; today she beguiles bike riders and other passersby.

land und Österreich ist. Nur das linke Ufer gehört noch zu Deutschland; die Donau hat nun 658 Kilometer zurückgelegt. Am jenseitigen Ufer breitet sich der oberösterreichische Donauraum aus.

Noch ein paar großzügige Kehren und die Donau erreicht den Jochenstein, einen Quarzfelsen inmitten des Flusses, der auch dem Kraftwerk und einer Schleuse sowie am deutschen Ufer der Burgruine Altjochenstein den Namen gab. Unter dem Felsen soll die Nixe Isa hausen und singend die Schiffsleute betören, sodass sie an dem Felsen mit ihren Schiffen zerschellen. Das Abbild der Nixe steht in Holz geschnitzt am linken Donauufer. Sie ist nicht die einzige Nixenskulptur, aber die letzte auf deutschem Boden. Die Donau verlässt kurz hinter der Jochensteiner Schleuse das Land und erreicht Österreich.

meters (18 miles) or so. Only the left bank is still part of Germany, and the Danube has 658 kilometers (409 miles) behind her. The Austrian Upper Danube region stretches out from the opposite bank.

After a few more expansive bends, the Danube reaches the Jochenstein, a quartz outcrop in the middle of the river that gave its name to the hydroelectric power plant and sluice nearby, as well as the ruins of Altjochenstein Castle. The mermaid Isa is said to live under the rock, beguiling shipmen with her singing until their ships are smashed to pieces on the rock. A carved wooden image of the mermaid stands on the left bank of the Danube. Hers is not the only mermaid sculpture on the Danube, but it is the last one on German soil. The river soon reaches Austria, leaving the Jochenstein sluice and Germany behind.

Die österreichische Donau

Am 1. Januar eines jeden Jahres stimmen die Wiener Philharmoniker im Goldenen Saal des Musikvereins – nachdem sie den Zuschauern ein fröhliches „Prosit Neujahr" zugerufen haben – als zweite Zugabe Johann Strauss' wohl bekanntesten Walzer an: „An der schönen blauen Donau". Der Donauwalzer wurde 1867 komponiert und begründete einen Mythos, der sich hartnäckig in den Köpfen festgesetzt hat, dass nämlich die Donau in Österreich blau sei. Ein einziger Blick beim Überqueren der Grenze zeigt, dass sie sich ihr schlammiges Braun bewahrt hat. Nur bei ganz ausgezeichnetem Wetter, wenn sich der strahlende Himmel in ihren Fluten spiegelt, dann ist die Donau tatsächlich blau.

Der Donauwalzer – von Strauss zunächst als Faschingsstück komponiert und später rein instrumental unter dem heutigen Namen veröffentlicht – wurde rund 20 Jahre später

The Austrian Danube

On the first of January each year, after wishing the audience in the Large Hall of the Vienna Musikverein a happy "Prosit Neujahr," the Vienna Philharmonic launches into its second encore, Johann Strauss' most famous waltz, "The Blue Danube." Composed in 1867, the Danube waltz established the myth that the river is blue in Austria. This belief has become firmly entrenched in people's minds, although a single glance at the point where the river crosses the German-Austria border confirms that it is still a rather muddy brown. Only when the weather is perfect and the bright blue sky is reflected in its waters does the Danube actually look blue.

Strauss first wrote the waltz to be played during the pre-Lenten Carnival season, and later published a purely instrumental version under its current title. But it wasn't until twenty years later that Franz von Gernerth provided a text for it.

▾ Blau ist die Donau – wie hier in Wien – auch in Österreich nur dann, wenn sich ein wolkenloser Himmel in ihren Wellen spiegelt. Ihre eigene Farbe ist Schlammbraun.
▾ Even in Austria, the Danube is only blue—as here in Vienna—when a cloudless sky is reflected in her waves: her true color is muddy brown.

von Franz von Gernerth neu betextet. „Donau so blau“ heißt sein Gedicht, das zusammen mit Strauss' Walzertakten zur heimlichen Hymne Österreichs avancierte:

„Donau so blau,
Durch Tal und Au
Wogst ruhig du dahin,
Dich grüßt unser Wien,
Dein silbernes Band
Knüpft Land an Land,
Und fröhliche Herzen schlagen
An deinem schönen Strand.“

Lässt man die Farbe einmal außer Acht, so ist an dem Gedicht doch einiges wahr; vor allem, dass die Donau schön ist. In Österreich angekommen, wird sie zur Linken vom Mühlviertel, zur Rechten vom Sauwald eingeschlossen. Der teils dicht bewaldete, teils von Wiesen und Feldern bewachsene harte Granitboden der Landschaft wurde von der Donau zu einem tiefen Tal ausgewaschen. Enge Mäander ziehen sich durch die oberösterreichische Landschaft, von denen die Schlö-

◂ Die Schlögener Schlinge: Hier macht die Donau fast eine Kehrtwende.
◂ The Schlögen bend, where the Danube makes a nearly 180° turn

Gernerth's poem "Danube, so Blue," in combination with Strauss' waltz rhythm, has come to have the status of an Austrian national anthem:

Danube, so blue,
Through dale and lea,
You calmly sway.
Our Vienna greets you,
Your silver thread
Joins land to land,
And happy hearts beat
On your beautiful shores.

Leaving aside the question of color for a moment, the poem is in some ways quite accurate. First and foremost, the Danube is certainly beautiful. Having arrived in Austria, she is enclosed by the Mühlviertel region on the left and the sylvan Sauwald on the right. The hard granite ground, thickly forested in places and covered with fields and meadows in others, has been carved into a deep valley by the Danube. The river makes tight loops as it moves through the Upper

▲ Nicht nur von großen Schubverbänden, auch von kleinen Motorbooten wird die Schlögener Schlinge befahren.
▲ Not only large barge trains navigate the Schlögen bend, but smaller motorboats as well.

gener Schlinge die wohl aufregendste ist. Zwischen den Flusskilometern 2181 und 2187 ändert die Donau zweimal ihre Fließrichtung um 180 Grad, nimmt plötzlich Kurs Richtung Nordwesten, um sich einige Kilometer später zurück nach Südosten zu wenden. Dabei bildet sich eine schmale Landzunge, deren umwaldete Spitze sogar bewirtschaftet wird. Die Donau rund um die Schlögener Schlinge wird intensiv genutzt: Mit ihrem modernen Yachthafen ist sie für die Motorbootsportler ebenso eine Verkehrsstraße wie für die europäische Frachtschifffahrt. Denn seit der Errichtung des 1964 fertiggestellten Aschacher Kraftwerks einige Kilometer flussabwärts staut sich die Donau hier. Ihr Pegel ist fast um das Doppelte gestiegen, und so ist der einst für die Schifffahrt so gefährliche Fluss zu einer idyllischen Wasserautobahn geworden.

Dem Fischreichtum hat der Bau des Kraftwerks und die damit verbundene Stauung erstaunlicherweise nicht geschadet:

Austrian landscape, and the sharp bend at Schlögen is surely the most exciting of all. Between kilometers 2,181 and 2,187 (miles 1,355 and 1,389), the river changes direction by 180 degrees twice: it suddenly takes a northwesterly course, only to turn back to the southeast a few kilometers later. A narrow tongue of land has formed in the process, and the tip, enclosed by woods, is even cultivated. The Danube is used intensively around the Schlögen bend. With its modern yacht harbor, it is a thoroughfare for motorboat sportsmen and European cargo ships alike. Since the completion of the Aschach power plant several kilometers downriver in 1964, the Danube has been dammed up here. The water level has doubled, and the river that was once so dangerous for boat travel has become an idyllic "water expressway."

Amazingly, construction of the power plant and the damming that came with it have not impacted the abundance

Über 60 Fischarten, darunter Zander, Braxe, Waller und Barbe, ziehen die Fischer mit ihren Netzen noch immer aus dem Fluss.

Die Wälder um die Donauschlinge herum sind ein Garten Eden: für Geologen, die hier – auf dem österreichischen Granit- und Gneisplateau – auf einem eigenen Naturlehrpfad geschult werden; für Radfahrer, die hier einmal von ihrem Rad absitzen und den Fluss vom Wasser aus genießen dürfen, oder für Wanderer, die durch intakte Wälder streifen können und neben Fichten auch Silberpappeln, Eschen und Eichen zu sehen bekommen.

Am Ende des engen bewaldeten Donautals passiert der Fluss das Kraftwerk von Aschach, um in eine dicht besiedelte und bewirtschaftete Ebene einzutreten. Die Donau nähert sich zunehmend der oberösterreichischen Landeshauptstadt Linz. Zuvor aber, kurz hinter Aschach, liegt am rechten Ufer etwas

of fish. Anglers can still pull more than sixty kinds of fish from the river, among them perch, bream, Wels catfish and barbel.

The wooded region surrounding the Danube bend are a Garden of Eden for geologists, who are schooled along their very own nature studies path on the Austrian granite and gneiss plateau. The same is true for bike riders, who can climb off their bikes and enjoy a dip in the river, and for hikers, who can roam through the pristine forest and spot white poplar, ash and oak trees among the plentiful spruce.

At the end of the thickly forested Danube Valley, the river passes the Aschach power plant as it enters the densely settled and cultivated plain. The Danube is drawing ever closer to the Austrian provincial capital of Linz. Just beyond Aschach bei Hartkirchen and prior to Linz, however, on the right bank

▾ In den lichten Wäldern von Sauwald und Mühlviertel rund um die Schlögener Schlinge
▾ In the lightly wooded Sauwald and Mühlviertel around the Schlögen bend

Sakristei

abseits die Burgruine Schaunberg, die einst – bevor sie ab dem 17. Jahrhundert dem Verfall preisgegeben wurde – mit einer Fläche von 17.500 Quadratmetern die größte Burgenanlage Oberösterreichs war. Von einer mächtigen Ringmauer umgeben, kann man heute noch die Hauptburg mit Teilen ihres Bergfrieds, des Palas und der Burgkapelle durchstreifen.

Unweit des anderen Donauufers bei Bad Mühllacken, beinahe auf gleicher Höhe von Burg Schaunberg, ließen die Herren von Oberwallsee – erbitterte Widersacher derer zu Schaunberg – ab 1364 die Burg Oberwallsee errichten. Auch sie ist heute nur noch Ruine.

Unbeschadet hat dagegen einige Flusskilometer weiter Schloss Ottensheim überstanden, ebenfalls aus einer mittelalterlichen Burg hervorgegangen. Doch das Schloss inmitten des gleichnamigen Örtchens ist in Privatbesitz und kann – anders als die beiden Ruinen – nicht besichtigt werden. Ottensheim selbst aber hat eine hübsche Altstadt und ist der drittälteste Markt Oberösterreichs.

and slightly out of the way, you can spot the ruins of Schaunberg Castle. With 17,500 square meters (188,000 square feet), it was the largest castle complex in Upper Austria before it was allowed to fall into disrepair beginning in the seventeenth century. Surrounded by a mighty ring wall, you can still wander through the main castle and parts of the keep, the great hall and the castle chapel.

The lords of Oberwallsee were archenemies of those at Schaunberg, and on the opposite bank of the Danube, not far from the river and near Bad Mühllacken, they had Oberwallsee Castle built almost parallel with Schaunberg. Today it, too, is nothing but a ruin.

Schloss Ottensheim, on the other hand, a few kilometers downriver, arose from a pre-existing medieval castle and is still intact. Located in the middle of a town by the same name, the palace is privately owned and, unlike the two ruins, cannot be visited. But Ottensheim itself has a charming old town and is the third oldest market town in Upper Austria.

◄ Die wahre Größe von Burg Schaunberg lässt sich in den Ruinen von Bergfried und Palas nur noch erahnen.
◄ The ruins of the castle keep and great hall only hint at the true size of Schaunberg Castle.
▼ Vom jenseitigen Donauufer eröffnet sich dem Betrachter von Ottensheim das sehr stimmige Bild eines alten Marktfleckens.
▼ From the opposite bank of the Danube, Ottensheim presents onlookers with a lovely and orderly image of an old market town.

In der oberösterreichischen Landeshauptstadt Linz angekommen, sollte man sich zuallererst ausgiebig dem unbestrittenen Star der Stadt widmen: der Linzer Torte. Das Gebäck aus haselnussverfeinertem Teig, Ribiselmarmelade – also Marmelade von roten Johannisbeeren – und einem gewürzten Teiggitter kauft man traditionell beim Konditor Wrann, in der k.u.k. Hofbäckerei oder einer der vielen anderen Bäckereien. Zwar kommen – sehr zum Unwillen der Linzer Bürger – seit Neuestem Gerüchte auf, die Linzer Torte stamme gar nicht aus der Stadt, sondern sei von einem Wiener Bäcker namens Linzer erfunden worden. Doch wer mag über solche Nichtigkeiten nachdenken, wenn er in Linz mit dem feinen Gebäck so wohlversorgt wird.

Linz ist eine Stadt mit zwei Gesichtern: die Moderne schiebt sich mehr und mehr in den historischen Kern hinein – vor allem auch kulturell. Nicht zufällig war die Stadt im Jahr 2009 zusammen mit Litauens Hauptstadt Vilnius Kulturhauptstadt Europas. Zu verdanken hat sie das auch der Vergangenheit: Seit der Frühzeit besiedelt, genoss die Stadt im Mittelalter Stapelrecht, was bis heute nachgewirkt hat. Kaufleute, die im Mittelalter die Donau hinauf- oder hinabfuhren, mussten in Linz haltmachen, ihre Ware ausladen und eine Weile zum Verkauf

Having arrived in Linz, capital of the state (or province) of Upper Austria, the first order of business is to devote some time to the undisputed star of the city, the Linzer Torte. Featuring a hazelnut-enhanced dough, red currant marmalade and a lattice of spiced dough, this cake is traditionally sold at pastry shops like the Konditorei Wrann, the k.u.k. Hofbäckerei ("Dual Monarchy Royal Bakery"), or one of the many other bakeries. Much to the dismay of the people of Linz, rumors have arisen recently that the Linzer Torte didn't originate here, but may have been invented by a Viennese baker named Linzer instead. But why waste time pondering such trivial matters when there's such an abundant supply of the fabulous cake in Linz?

Linz is a city with two faces. Modernity has increasingly crept into the historical core, particularly on the cultural front. It is no coincidence that the city was named the 2009 Cultural Capital of Europe, along with the Lithuanian capital of Vilnius. But Linz also has the past to thank for its rich heritage. Inhabited since prehistoric times, the city was accorded the medieval staple right, which still has an impact today. During the Middle Ages, traders who traveled up and down the Danube were required to stop in Linz, unload their wares and

▾ Blick auf das winterliche Linz. Im Hintergrund der Pöstlingberg – Wahrzeichen der Stadt – mit seiner Basilika.

▾ A view of Linz in wintertime: in the background is the Pöstlingberg, symbol of the city, with its basilica.

anbieten. Das machte die Stadt nicht nur reich, sie brauchte auch einen großen Hafen – und den hat sie noch heute. Es ist der größte Hafen Österreichs und überhaupt in der Region der oberen Donau. Knapp vier Millionen Tonnen Güter werden auf dem etwa 150 Hektar großen Gelände jährlich umgeschlagen. In Linz wird dem Besucher denn auch endgültig klar, dass die Donau für den Güterverkehr Europas unverzichtbar geworden ist. Die Fracht der riesigen Lastkähne und Schubverbände wäre über Schienen nicht mehr zu bewältigen. Für die Ökologie der Donau war dies jahrzehntelang eine Katastrophe, vor allem durch die riesigen Tanklager. Nach mehreren Schadensfällen an den Tanks der 1960er- und 70er-Jahre wird der Tankhafen saniert.

Doch Linz kann sich auch von anderer Seite zeigen: Das Wahrzeichen der Stadt, die Wallfahrtskirche „Basilika Sieben Schmerzen Mariae“, der der Papst 1964 den Ehrentitel Basilica minor verlieh, strahlt ihren barocken Glanz vom Pöstlingberg über das gesamte Linz aus. Der Berg ist aber vor allem wegen der Linzer Grottenbahn, einer Art Märchenpark auf Schienen, eines der beliebtesten Ausflugsziele der Städter. Zu diesen gehört auch die Donaulände, der Donaupark am Südufer der Donau, in der das Brucknerhaus für erstklassige

offer them for sale. This not only made the city wealthy, but also necessitated a large harbor—which Linz still has today. In fact, the city has the largest harbor in Austria and in the entire Upper Danube region. Almost four million tons of goods are transshipped annually through the approximately 150-hectare (371-acre) harbor area. Here in Linz it becomes clear once and for all that the Danube has become indispensable for the transport of goods throughout Europe. The volume of freight carried on huge cargo barges and barge trains could not be handled by rail. For decades, this was catastrophic for the ecology of the Danube, particularly due to the enormous fuel storage depots. After several instances of damage to the tanks, the tank harbor was overhauled in the 1960s and 1970s.

But Linz has another side as well. The city's landmark is the pilgrimage basilica that exudes its baroque splendor over all of Linz from atop the Pöstlingberg. Dedicated to the Seven Sorrows of Our Lady, the pope designated the church a minor basilica in 1964. The mountain is a favorite destination for residents of the city, not least because of the Linz Grottenbahn, or cave railway, a kind of underground fairy-tale park on rails. Other attractions include the Donaulände (known locally as the Danube Park) on the south shore of the river, top-notch

Exkurs: Das KZ Mauthausen

Es waren die Granitvorkommen in der Nähe des oberösterreichischen Mauthausen, die 1938, nach dem Anschluss Österreichs an Deutschland, für die Nazis so interessant waren, dass sie dort ein Konzentrationslager errichteten. Die Häftlinge konnten so als billige Arbeitskräfte in den dortigen Steinbrüchen eingesetzt und politische und andere Gegner gleichzeitig ausgeschaltet werden. Indem im August des Jahres 1938 die ersten 300 Sträflinge – der SS-Kategorien „kriminell" oder „asozial" angehörend – aus dem KZ Dachau nach Mauthausen deportiert wurden, wurde eines der furchtbarsten Kapitel in der Geschichte des österreichischen Donauraumes geschrieben: Etwa 200.000 Menschen aus allen europäischen Ländern waren hier und in mehreren Außenlagern zwischen 1938 und 1945 inhaftiert, von denen die Hälfte ermordet wurde.

Excursion: The Mauthausen Concentration Camp

There was granite was to be found in the vicinity of Mauthausen in Upper Austria. After Germany annexed Austria in 1938, the rock was so important to the Nazis that they built a concentration camp there. Prisoners could be used as cheap labor in the rock quarries, and at the same time, political opponents and other undesirables could be disposed of.

The first 300 prisoners, categorized by the SS as "criminal" or "antisocial," were deported from the concentration camp at Dachau to Mauthausen in August 1938. Thus began one of the most terrible chapters in the history of the Austrian Danube region. Between 1938 and 1945, around 200,000 people from every country in Europe were interned here and in several outlying camps. Half of them were murdered.

▼ Das Denkmal für die italienischen Ermordeten im KZ Mauthausen, der heutigen KZ-Gedenkstätte Mauthausen
▼ The monument to the Italians killed in the Mauthausen concentration camp, today the site of the Mauthausen KZ Monument

Selbst für KZ-Maßstäbe galt Mauthausen als eines der grausamsten Konzentrationslager überhaupt. Nicht wenige Häftlinge überstanden – ausgezehrt vom Transport und meist einer vorangegangenen Haft – kaum die Prozedur der Aufnahme: Stundenlang unbekleidet Appell stehen, anschließend die Desinfektion, Einkleidung und Registrierung, nicht zu vergessen die Schikanen, Schläge und Demütigungen der SS-Leute überlebte regelmäßig nur ein kleiner Teil der Gefangenen. Wer übrig blieb, wurde den Baracken und Arbeitsgruppen zugeteilt, und das grausige Leben im KZ begann.

Die Haftbedingungen waren entsetzlich, der Tag von der Arbeit im Steinbruch, ab 1943 auch in der Rüstungsindustrie strukturiert. Mauthausen war ein „Todeslager", und neben den Erschießungen, Erhängungen, Vergasungen und dem Tod infolge von Folter, Hunger und Krankheit waren manche Arbeiten im Steinbruch geradezu darauf ausgelegt, die Häftlinge damit zu töten. Dazu gehörte die Todesstiege, eine Treppe mit 186 ungleichmäßig hohen Stufen, die den Steinbruch mit dem eigentlichen KZ verband. Über sie musste die Strafkompanie, also die Häftlinge, die ermordet werden sollten, die Granitblöcke tragen – eine Arbeit, die auf Dauer niemand überleben konnte. Fast alle jüdischen Häftlinge wurden als Steineträger eingesetzt, aber auch „politische", „kriminelle" und „asoziale" Häftlinge fanden bei dieser Arbeit den Tod. Die Granitblöcke mussten zur Donau getragen werden, von wo aus sie verschifft wurden.

Die Befreiung des Konzentrationslagers Mauthausen begann in der Nacht vom 2. zum 3. Mai 1945, in der die SS-Mannschaften das Lager verließen und die Wiener Feuerschutzpolizei zunächst die Häftlingsbewachung übernahm. Zwei Tage später, am 5. Mai, trafen erste Einheiten der US-Armee ein, und die Häftlinge übernahmen die Kontrolle über das gesamte Lager. Heute sind das Gelände des Konzentrationslagers und des Steinbruchs eine Mahn- und Gedenkstätte. Denkmäler erinnern an die Häftlinge der zahlreichen Nationalitäten. Das Besucherzentrum der Stätte hütet außerdem eine große Anzahl an Zeitzeugenberichten, die man sich vor Ort ansehen kann. Vom KZ selbst sind noch das Haupttor, wenige Baracken und auch die umgestaltete Todesstiege zu sehen. Auf dem Appellplatz wurde als zentrales Monument ein Sarkophag errichtet, dessen lateinische Inschrift „Aus der Toten Geschick mögen lernen die Lebenden" die nachfolgenden Generationen mahnt. Im ehemaligen Gebäude der Wäscherei wurde ein Weiheraum und eine Kapelle eingerichtet.

Even by KZ standards, Mauthausen was one of the most gruesome of all concentration camps. Debilitated by travel, and in most cases from prior imprisonment, many prisoners barely survived the admissions process. They stood naked for hours during roll call, followed by disinfection, outfitting and registration, to say nothing of the harrassment, physical blows and humiliation they suffered at the hands of the SS. Often, only a small portion of the newly arrived prisoners survived. Those who did were assigned to the barracks and work groups, and the horrific life of the KZ began.

Conditions in the camps were appalling. The days were built around work in the quarry and, beginning in 1943, manufacturing weapons. Mauthausen was a death camp: in addition to executions by shooting, hangings, gassings and deaths resulting from torture, hunger and disease, many jobs in the quarry were virtually designed with the intention of killing the prisoners. Among them was the Stairway of Death, a staircase with 186 steps of irregular height that connected the actual KZ to the quarry. The punishment battalion, that is to say, the prisoners who were to be murdered, had to carry granite blocks up the staircase. No one could survive at this task for long. Nearly all the Jews were used as rock carriers, but prisoners categorized as political, criminal and asocial also worked themselves to death this way. The granite blocks had to be carried to the Danube and were shipped from there.

The liberation of the Mauthausen concentration camp began on the night of May 2-3, 1945. The SS units left the camp that night, and Viennese firefighters guarded the prisoners for a time. Two days later, on May 5, the first units of the U.S. Army arrived and the prisoners took control of the entire camp.

Today, the concentration camp and quarry are memorial sites. Monuments remind us of prisoners from many nations. The on-site visitor center also houses a large number of reports by contemporary witnesses, which people can view there. Visitors can still see the main gate, a few of the barracks, and the redesigned Stairway of Death. On the parade ground where roll was taken, a sarcophagus was erected as a central monument, bearing a Latin inscription that warns future generations: "May the living learn from the fate of the dead." A shrine and chapel have been established in the former laundry building.

Konzerte und das Lentos Kunstmuseum für eine Kunstsammlung von Weltrang stehen.

Von der Umgebung rund um Linz ist man hin- und hergerissen: Auf der einen Seite kann man von den Hügeln rundumher an klaren Tagen die Alpengipfel bewundern, die auch im Sommer häufig noch strahlend weiß verschneit sind. Auf der anderen Seite aber präsentiert sich der Fluss recht urban. Er ist, auch wenn er in den Grenzen der weiten natürlichen Mäander verläuft, stark begradigt, der Uferbewuchs keinesfalls mehr der der natürlichen Auwälder. Die Schäden an der Natur sind offensichtlich – immer mal wieder trifft man auf abgestorbene Bäume.

Weit schwerwiegendere Auswirkungen hat die Eindämmung jedoch auf die Fließgeschwindigkeit der Donau und die Absenkung des Grundwasserspiegels. Wenn die Donau hinter Linz in das weite Marchland – die Kornkammer Österreichs – eintritt, so wird das Gebiet zwar durch die Donauregulierung seltener von Hochwasser heimgesucht, ein weiteres Absinken

concerts performed at the Brucknerhaus and the world-class collection of the Lentos Art Museum.

Visitors may well be torn about how to spend their time in the Linz area. On clear days, the hills around the town provide beautiful panoramic views of the peaks of the Alps, which are often covered in gleaming white snow, even in summer. The river, on the other hand, has a more urbane aspect to it. Although it flows within the borders of its wide, naturally winding course, the river has been intensely regulated. The vegetation alongs its banks is no longer anything like the natural riverside woods. The damage inflicted on nature is evident, and dead trees are not an uncommon sight.

But the damming of the Danube has had much more serious consequences for the river's flow rate and lowering of its water level. When the Danube enters the wide marchland beyond Linz, known as Austria's breadbasket, the area is ravaged by flooding much less often, yet further lowering of the water level could have disastrous consequences. That is why citizens

▾ Nicht überall an der Donau ist die Natur noch intakt.
▾ The natural world is not intact along every part of the Danube.

▾ Das Gotteshaus von Mitterkirchen
▾ A house of worship in the town of Mitterkirchen

des Grundwasserspiegels könnte dort aber katastrophale Folgen haben. Gegen weitere Regulierungen wehren sich Bürger und Umweltverbände daher vehement. Vorbei an Mauthausen, Mitterkirchen – einem hübschen Örtchen, in dessen Nähe ein Gräberfeld der Hallstatt-Kultur entdeckt wurde – und schließlich Grein fließt die Donau in den Strudengau. Das enge schmale Tal, auch heute noch schön zu durchfahren, war einst für die Schiffer eine der gefährlichsten Abschnitte der österreichischen Donau überhaupt: Felsnadeln ragten in die Fahrrinne, gefährliche Strudel ließen so manches Schiff vom Weg abkommen. Mittlerweile wurde auch dieser Teil begradigt, gefährliche Felsen weggesprengt, und die Donau fließt recht gemächlich.

Der Strom bildet bereits seit Mauthausen die Grenze zwischen Oberösterreich (linkes Ufer) und Niederösterreich (rechtes Ufer), und in Niederösterreich beginnt bei Ardagger noch vor dem Strudengau das sogenannte Mostviertel. Der Name lässt durchaus Rückschlüsse auf die Nutzung der Gegend zu: Auf saftigen Streuobstwiesen wachsen hier vor allem

and environmental groups are vehemently opposed to any additional regulation of the river. The Danube flows past Mauthausen, Mitterkirchen and finally Grein, entering the Strudengau district. Mitterkirchen is a pretty little town, and a Hallstatt-culture burial ground has been discovered right nearby. This narrow little valley, still a lovely place to sail through today, was once the most dangerous section of the Austrian Danube for shippers. Sharp rocks jutted up in the shipping lane, and dangerous whirlpools caused many a boat to go astray. In the meantime, this section has also been improved. Dangerous rocks were blown up, and the Danube now flows at a rather leisurely pace.

Beginning in Mauthausen, the river forms the border between Upper Austria on the left bank and Lower Austria on the right. In Lower Austria, the area called the *Mostviertel* ("must region") begins near Ardagger, prior to the Strudengau district. The name suggests what goes on here: the juice pears for which the area is famous are the main attraction, but apples also grow in the lush meadows scattered with fruit

▾ Streuobstwiesen im österreichischen Mostviertel
▾ Meadows scattered with fruit trees in the region of Austrian famous for its fruit wines

die berühmten Mostbirnen, aber auch Äpfel. In sogenannten Mostheurigen und Jausen wird die Tradition des Mosttrinkens noch immer allerorten gepflegt, und man sollte sich die Gelegenheit nicht entgehen lassen, reinen Birnenmost – eine Spezialität der Gegend – zu verkosten.

Mit dem Strudengau kehrt die Donau der Industrie nach und nach den Rücken, noch muss sie das Kraftwerk bei Ybbs-Persenbeug überwinden, doch dann trifft sie auf die weichen Hügel des Nibelungengaus, dessen Name auf Rüdiger von Bechelaren, heute Pöchlarn, einem Getreuen des Hunnenkönigs Etzels im Nibelungenlied, zurückgeht. Dort kommt bald die Wallfahrtskirche Maria Taferl hoch über der Donau in Sicht. Bereits die Kelten hatten hier einen Opferstein, den man noch im Kirchhof besichtigen kann; die frühen Christen nutzten die weihevolle Atmosphäre für ihre Zwecke und errichteten die – in späteren Jahrhunderten immer wieder umgebaute – Basilika. Wenige Kilometer hinter dem Wallfahrtsort erreicht die Donau den vorläufigen Höhepunkt ihrer Österreichreise: die Wachau. Nur rund 30 Flusskilometer ist dieser Donaudurch-

trees. The tradition of drinking newly fermented wines is still alive and well in taverns and pubs everywhere. Whatever you do, don't miss the chance to taste pure pear wine, a local specialty, at least once.

When it enters the Strudengau, the Danube gradually turns its back on industry. The river must still pass the Ybbs-Persenbeug power plant, but then it meets the soft hills of the Nibelungengau. The name of this district goes back to Rüdiger von Bechelaren (today Pöchlarn), who was a loyal follower of Etzel, king of the Huns, in the Nibelungenlied. This is where the pilgrimage church of Maria Taferl comes into view high above the Danube. The Celts already had a sacrificial stone here, and it is still displayed in the churchyard. Early Christians used the solemn atmosphere for their own purposes and built this basilica, which has been renovated and rebuilt quite a few times in the succeeding centuries. A few kilometers beyond the pilgrimage church, the Danube reaches a high point of its Austrian journey, at least for now: the Wachau. This gap breaks through the hard granite and gneiss

▾ Die Wallfahrtskirche Maria Taferl im Donaunebel
▾ The pilgrimage church of Maria Taferl in the Danube fog

▲ Eine Schiffsreise durch die Wachau – mit Sicherheit eines der schönsten Donauerlebnisse
▲ A boat trip through the Wachau is surely one of the finest experiences to be had on the Danube.

bruch durch das harte Granit- und Gneishochland lang, und doch sammelt sich dort eine solche Vielfalt an Kultur- und Naturgut, dass die Landschaft im Jahr 2000 zusammen mit ihrer reichen Anzahl an Kulturgütern zum UNESCO-Welterbe ernannt wurde. Die Wachau erstreckt sich beidseits des Flusses und liegt am linken Ufer im Waldviertel, am rechten im Dunkelsteinerwald.

Das imposante, seit dem 11. Jahrhundert bestehende Benediktinerstift Melk, das hoch über der Donau thront, bildet das Tor zur Wachau und präsentiert sich heute in einem barocken „Neubau". Die riesige Klosteranlage bildet nicht nur die größte ihresgleichen in Österreich, sie gilt auch als die schönste und prächtigste. Vom National Geographic Traveler Magazin wurde das Stift im November 2008 zur „Best Historic Destination in the World" gekürt. Die Juroren begründeten ihre Entscheidung damit, dass die Anlage nicht nur schön und hervorragend erhalten sei, sondern die Führung durch das Barockensemble auch so lebendig sei, dass man sich tat-

mountains surrounding the Danube for a distance of only 30 km (18.5 miles), yet the area encompasses such a variety of cultural and natural assets that the landscape and its cultural resources were granted UNESCO World Heritage status in 2000. The Wachau Valley stretches along both sides of the river, with the Waldviertel on the left and the Dunkelstein Forest on the right.

The imposing Benedictine Abbey of Melk has towered high above the Danube since the eleventh century, forming the gateway to the Wachau Valley. The abbey currently presents a "newly constructed" baroque face. The enormous monastic complex is the largest of its kind in Austria, as well as the most beautiful and resplendent. In November 2008, *National Geographic Traveler Magazine* chose Melk as the "Best Historic Destination in the World."

Not only is the complex beautiful and outstandingly preserved, jurors wrote explaining their decision, but the guided

sächlich in die Vergangenheit zurückversetzt fühle. Und in der Tat: Ist die weithin sichtbare Anlage schon rein äußerlich beeindruckend, so versetzt einen der Gang durch das Kloster mit dem Kolomanihof, der Stiftskirche und dem überwältigenden Marmorsaal immer wieder in Erstaunen. Letzterer war der Speisesaal für vornehme Gäste des Klosters – unter anderem für das Kaiserhaus – und wurde mit Adneter und Untersberger Marmor ausgestattet. Bei der Besichtigung sollte man vor allem den Blick zur Decke heben: Das herrliche Deckenfresko von Paul Troger ist von der Architekturmalerei Gaetano Fantis umgeben, die dort Tiefe und Wölbung vortäuscht, wo die Decke eben ist.

Doch was seit Jahrhunderten ein kulturelles Zentrum des ehemaligen Kaiserreichs war, war – und ist – noch weit mehr ein geistiges Zentrum. Und so verwundert es nicht, dass die Räume der Bibliothek von Melk die eindrucksvollsten der ganzen Anlage sind. Auch hier hat Paul Troger das Deckenfresko gemalt, aber anders als im Marmorsaal bleibt es beim Anblick von Tausenden von Büchern in prachtvollen, blattgoldverzierten Holzregalen beinahe unbeachtet. In insgesamt

◀ Kloster Melk – Wahrzeichen der Wachau
◀ Melk Abbey: landmark of the Wachau Valley

tours through the baroque "ensemble" were so vivid that people actually felt as if they'd been transported back in time. And it's true: while the abbey is already impressive from the exterior, and it is visible from quite a distance, a stroll through the monastery with its Benedictine Hall, the abbey church and the stupendous Marble Hall will leave you in awe.

The latter was a refectory for the monastery's distinguished guests, among them members of the imperial dynasty, and was furnished with Adnet and Untersberg marble. Don't forget to admire the refectory ceiling. The exquisite ceiling fresco by Paul Troger is surrounded by Gaetano Fanti's architectural painting, which simulates depth and vaulting where the ceiling is actually flat.

They abbey that served as a cultural center of the former Austrian Empire for centuries was, and still is, to an even greater degree a spiritual center. So it is not surprising that Melk Abbey's library contains some of the most spectacular rooms in the entire complex. Here, too, Paul Toger painted the ceiling fresco, but unlike in the Marble Hall, it goes almost

▲ Auf den Granitfelsen der Wachau errichtet: Schloss Schönbühel
▲ Schloss Schönbühel was built on the granite rocks of the Wachau.

zwölf Räumen ruht die Weisheit von rund 750 Inkunabeln, 1700 Werken aus dem 16., 4500 aus dem 17. und 18.000 aus dem 18. Jahrhundert – zusammen mit neueren Büchern sind es insgesamt um die 100.000 Bände, zu denen noch einmal 1888 Handschriften hinzukommen. Deren älteste stammt aus dem 9. Jahrhundert. Die Melker Bibliothek zählt zu den ältesten der Welt und wird von den Benediktinern und eventuellen gelehrten Gästen noch immer genutzt – ein Ort der Gelehrsamkeit, der leider nicht in allen Teilen besichtigt werden kann.

Es fällt schwer, sich von Stift Melk zu verabschieden, doch dahinter lockt die Wachau mit einigen weiteren Freuden – geistiger, kultureller, aber vor allem auch profan-weltlicher, genussreicher Art. Ein paar Meter das enge Felsental der Wachau mit dem Schiff befahrend, weiß man kaum noch, wohin man seinen Blick wenden soll. Melk hat man hinter

unnoticed among the thousands of books in their magnificent, ornate wooden bookshelves decorated with gold leaf. Residing in twelve rooms is the wisdom of around 750 incunabula (books written before 1501), 1,700 works from the sixteenth century, 4,500 from the seventeenth and 18,000 from the eighteenth. Along with newer books, the collection totals about 100,000 volumes. Added to that are 1,888 manuscripts, the oldest of which dates back to the ninth century. The Melk Library is among the oldest in the world, and is still used by the Benedictines and on occasion by scholarly visitors. Unfortunately, not all areas of this place of learning are open to the public.

It is hard to say goodbye to Melk Abbey, but the Wachau beckons with further delights, including spiritual, cultural and, above all, earthly pleasures. Traveling just a short way further in the narrow, rocky valley of the Wachau by ship, it's

sich gelassen, da folgt das kleine Schlösschen Schönbühel, direkt auf den Granitfelsen am rechten Donauufer erbaut. Und so geht es in einem fort. Das schneeweiße Servitenkloster taucht auf, 1675 ebenfalls auf dem Granit errichtet und in seiner Architektur von der Geburtskirche in Bethlehem inspiriert. Nur ein weniges weiter und die Wachaufelsen werden von der Burgruine Aggstein überragt: Dort soll einst der grausame Raubritter Georg Scheck vom Walde, genannt Ritter Schreckenwald, gehaust haben. Seine vielen Gefangenen ließ er in einer tiefen Felsspalte festsetzen und ließ ihnen die Wahl, wie sie sterben wollten: durch Verhungern oder einen raschen Sprung die Donauklippen hinab. In den heute romantischen Burgruinen kann sogar geheiratet werden – die mittelalterliche Kapelle steht noch.

Kleine malerische Orte liegen dazwischen, und am Ufer der Donau – und manchmal auch etwas abseits davon – führt

hard to know where to look first. Melk is behind you, but it is followed by Schloss Schönbühel, a small castle built directly atop the granite rocks on the right bank of the Danube. And there is more. A little further on, the ruins of Aggstein Castle tower over the Wachau rock formations.

The dreadful robber baron Georg Scheck vom Walde, called the "terror of the forest," supposedly lived in the castle at one time. He had his many prisoners thrown into a deep cleft and let them decide whether they would rather die by starvation or with a quick jump off the Danube cliffs. Today, couples can actually be married in the romantic castle ruins: the medieval chapel still stands.

There are plenty of picturesque spots in between, and alongside the Danube—sometimes a short distance away from the river—runs the Danube Bike Trail. The bike path

▾ Von seiner Burg Aggstein aus hatte Raubritter Scheck vom Walde einst die Donau fest im Griff.
▾ The robber baron, Scheck vom Walde, once had the Danube firmly under his control from his Aggstein Castle.

▲ Der Donauradweg führt durch eine abwechslungsreiche Landschaft.
▲ The Danube bike path travels through a rich variety of landscapes.

▲ Grüner Veltliner und Riesling wachsen am besten auf dem Granit der Wachau.
▲ Grüner Veltliner and Riesling grapes grow best on the granite of the Wachau.

noch immer der Donauradweg. Er begleitet die Donau zwar auf ihrem gesamten Weg, doch ist er zwischen Passau und Wien und insbesondere in der Wachau am stärksten befahren. Der Donauradweg verläuft nicht auf seiner gesamten Länge beidseitig der Donau, immer wieder einmal müssen die Radfahrer die Seiten wechseln. Doch hier, in der Wachau, kann man sich die Strecke aussuchen – und wäre doch nie damit bestraft, nur ein Donauufer zur Verfügung zu haben. Denn beidseits des Flusses erstrecken sich nun die steilen, ab etwa 800 n. Chr. errichteten und bewirtschafteten Weinterrassen. Es ist eine mühevolle Arbeit, die schmalen, stark abschüssigen Hänge zu beackern. In erster Linie gedeihen hier weiße Rebsorten, Grüner Veltliner und Riesling. Aus ihnen werden in der Wachau aromatisch-frische und sehr fruchtbetonte Weine erzeugt.

Zu verdanken ist dies dem einzigartigen Klima: Fröste und die kalten Winde aus Dunkelsteinerwald und Waldviertel

actually accompanies the Danube along its entire length, but sees the greatest amount of traffic between Passau and Vienna, especially in the Wachau. The Danube bike path does not extend along both sides of the river for it entire distance, so bike riders have to repeatedly change sides. Here in the Wachau, though, you can choose your route without ever being punished by having only one side of the Donau at your disposal. That's because the steep wine terraces, first planted and cultivated around 800 CE, spread out on both sides of this stretch of the river. Working on the steep, narrow slopes is an arduous task. White grapes such as Grüner Veltliner and Riesling are the main varieties that thrive here. The fresh, aromatic and very fruity wines of the Wachau are made from these grapes.

Their success is the result of the area's unique climate. The rapid flow of the Danube moderates the frosts and cold winds that come from the Dunkelstein Forest and Wald-

werden durch die hohe Fließgeschwindigkeit der Donau gemildert und relativ zügig „abtransportiert". Gleichzeitig sorgen die Winde für eine fortwährende frische Belüftung der Weinberge. Das Terroir – vor allem das verwitterte Granit-Gneis-Gemisch der Felshänge – ist ideal für den Riesling und mehr noch für den Grünen Veltliner. Letzterer war jahrzehntelang das Stiefkind der Weinkenner, man beurteilte die Rebsorte als allenfalls alltagstauglich und für Straußenwirtschaften geeignet. Heute leisten auch die schärfsten Kritiker Abbitte, wenn sie einen der hochkarätigen Wachauer Veltliner verkosten: Die alterungsfähigen Gewächse beeindrucken durch ihre Mineralität, Komplexität und ausgewogene Stuktur. Neben dem Verwitterungsgestein der Wachau und den Winden sind dafür auch die erheblich schwankenden Temperaturen zwischen Tag und Nacht sowie das Wärmereservoir der Donau verantwortlich. Auch der Wachauer Riesling hat diesen Bedingungen seine Eleganz und Kraft zu verdanken.

Auch wenn die Wachau eigentlich ein flächenmäßig eher kleines Gebiet umfasst, werden durch die Steinterrassen, die

viertel, carrying them away at a rather brisk tempo. At the same time, the winds ensure that fresh air flows through the vineyards continuously. The terroir, particularly the granite-gneiss soil of the rocky slopes, is ideal for Riesling and even more so for Grüner Veltliner. For decades, the latter was the "stepchild" of wine connoisseurs, who judged the grape varietal suitable at best for everyday consumption or for new wine consumed on the winegrowers' premises. Today, however, even the sharpest critics apologize when they taste top-quality Wachau Veltliner. The minerality, complexity and well-balanced structure of the wine ensure that it ages well. In addition to the winds and the rocky soil of the Wachau, two other factors are responsible for these qualities: the heat reservoir of the Danube and the considerable differences between daytime and nighttime temperatures. Wachau Rieslings owe their elegance and strength to these conditions as well.

Even though the Wachau comprises a rather small area, the stone terraces take advantage of every last bit of the

▾ Die Weinberge der Wachau bezaubern auch durch ihre zarte Blumen- und Tierwelt.
▾ The Wachau vineyards are also captivating due to their delicate flora and fauna.

auch den letzten Flecken Hang ausnutzen, insgesamt 1400 Hektar für den Weinbau genutzt. Davon wird auf mehr als der Hälfte, nämlich etwa 720 Hektar, Grüner Veltliner kultiviert, 190 Hektar sind für den Riesling reserviert. Den Rest müssen sich Rebsorten wie Müller-Thurgau, Sauvignon blanc, Muscateller und wenige Rotweinsorten teilen. Organisiert sind die meisten Winzer in der Vereinigung Vinea Wachau Nobilis Districtus, die auch eigene Weinprädikate eingeführt hat: „Federspiel", „Steinfeder" und „Smaragd" nennen sich die Prädikate, beziehen sich auf das Mostgewicht der zu kelternden Trauben sowie auf Alkoholgehalt und Restsüße des Weins und tragen die Namen eines Trainingsgeräts für Jagdfalken, einer auf den Terrassen heimischen Grasart und der auffällig tiefgrünen Smaragdeidechse.

slopes, and a total of 1,400 hectares (3,460 acres) are used for grape cultivation. More than half of that, around 720 hectares (1,779 acres) is devoted to Grüner Veltliner grapes, while about 190 hectares (470 acres) are reserved for Riesling. The rest has to be shared among Müller-Thurgau, Sauvignon blanc, and a few red grape varieties. Most of the local vintners belong to the Vinea Wachau Nobilis Districtus association, which has introduced quality-tested wines in three classifications based on the must weight of the pressed grapes, as well as the alcohol and residual sugar content of the wine: Federspiel, Steinfeder, and Smaragd. They are named for a device used in training hunting falcons, a type of grass native to the terraces, and the conspicuously dark green "emerald" lizard, respectively.

▸ „Goldner funkelt hier die Sonne ... In den Bergen der Wachau", meint ein österreichischer Heimatdichter.
▸ "The sun shines more brightly here – in the hills of the Wachau," according to one local Austrian poet.
▾ In den grünen Weinbergen der Wachau
▾ In the green vineyards of the Wachau

Die unzähligen Heurigenlokale laden in der Wachau dazu ein, sich mit dem Thema Wein ein bisschen näher zu beschäftigen. Die echten Heurigenlokale – eigentlich Buschenschank genannt – verkaufen dabei nur Wein und Schnaps aus eigener Herstellung, bieten ausschließlich (gesetzlich festgelegte) kalte Speisen und haben keine anderen alkoholischen Getränke auf der Karte. Sie sollte man in der Wachau auf jeden Fall einmal aufsuchen, sind sie doch noch wesentlich urtümlicher als andere Straußenwirtschaften und Weinlokale.

Die von dunklen Fichtenwäldern, die sich bis ans Donauufer hinabziehen, durchsetzte Kulturlandschaft wird auch auf dem Weiterweg immer wieder von Kirchen und Burgen unterbrochen. Das Örtchen Spitz liegt am linken Flussufer, die Ruine Hinterhaus direkt darüber. Der Ort befindet sich im Naturpark Jauerling; der Jauerling ist mit 960 Metern über Adria (wie in Österreich gemessen wird) der höchste Punkt der Wachau. Dem Naturpark gegenüber, am rechten Donauufer, erstreckt sich der Dunkelsteinerwald, und in beiden Gebieten

The countless *Heurigen* in the Wachau invite people to delve more deeply into the topic of wines. The genuine Heuriger taverns, actually called Buschenschänke, only sell wine and schnapps they themselves have produced in that same year. They also serve cold foods, as required by law, and have no other alcoholic beverages on their menus. Anyone visiting the Wachau should plan to visit one, because they still offer a considerably more authentic experience than winegrowers' tasting rooms and wine bars.

As we continue downstream, the cultural landscape, punctuated with dark pine forests that extend all the way to the banks of the Danube, continues to be dotted with churches and castles. The village of Spitz lies on the left bank of the river with the ruins of Hinterhaus Castle directly above it, and is located in the Jauerling Nature Preserve. Jauerling Mountain stands 960 meters (3,150 feet) above the Adriatic (the point from which elevation is measured in Austria) and is thus the highest point in the Wachau. Opposite the nature preserve, the

▾ An Burgen und Schlössern ist die Wachau reich: Hier bietet Burg Hinterhaus in Spitz eine malerische Kulisse.
▾ The Wachau boasts a wealth of castles and fortresses: here Hinterhaus Castle in Spitz provides a picturesque setting.

kann man in Form von Felsenmeeren, Felsnadeln oder Wackelsteinen ein typisches geologisches Phänomen des österreichischen Granit-Gneis-Hochlandes bewundern – die sogenannten Wollsackverwitterungen. Die gerundeten Kanten der Felsen entstehen nicht etwa durch Abrieb. Sie bilden sich, wenn in den recht grobkristallinen Graniten und Gneisen, solange sie unter der Bodenoberfläche ruhen, Risse und Spalten entstehen. Regenwasser dringt in diese Klüfte ein und zersetzt vor allem die Ecken und Kanten schneller als den Rest des Gesteins. So entstehen runde Verwitterungsformen, die wie weiche Wollsäcke oder Kissen aussehen. Das alles geschah in der Wachau im Tertiär, das mit dem Ende der Kreidezeit vor etwa 65 Millionen Jahren begann und vor etwa 2,6 Millionen Jahren endete. Nachdem durch Bodenerosion oder Klimaveränderungen die verwitterten Granit- und Gneisblöcke freigelegt wurden, ragen sie in ihrer heutigen Form aus ihrer Umgebung hervor, bilden mystisch anmutende Felsen und sind dadurch immer wieder Schauplatz unheimlicher Sagen und Legenden. Diese handeln von einer österreichischen Lorelei,

Dunkelstein Forest stretches out along the right bank of the Danube. Both areas feature felsenmeers (block fields), sharp rocky pinnacles and logan stones (rocking stones), geological formations characteristic of the Austrian granite and gneiss highlands. These formations result from a special pattern of weathering of rocks called *Wollsackverwitterung* in German, or "wool sack weathering." The rocks' rounded edges are not the result of abrasion. They come about when cracks and fissures form in the rather coarsely crystalline granite and gneiss while they are still under the earth's surface. Rainwater gets into the crevices and corrodes the corners and edges faster than the rest of the rock. And that is how round, weathered shapes that look like soft wool sacks or pillows formed. In the Wachau, this took place during the Tertiary period that began around 65 million years ago at the close of the Cretaceous period and ended around 2.6 million years ago. Ever since climate changes and erosion exposed the weathered granite and gneiss blocks, they have protruded from their surroundings, forming mystical rock formations that have often been

▾ Typische Wollsackverwitterungen in der Wachau
▾ Typical weathering of the rocks in the Wachau

▲ Eine der meistbesuchten Attraktionen der Wachau ist die Burgruine Dürnstein.
▲ The ruins of Dürnstein Castle are one of the region's main attractions.

die mit ihrem Gesang und ihren goldenen Haaren die Donauschiffer anlockt, sodass sie an den Wachaufelsen zerschellen, oder vom Teufel, der die Felsnadeln aufeinandertürmte – immer, um einem Menschen damit zu schaden. Eine berichtet auch von bösartigen Zwergen, die in den Felshöhlen hausten, dort ein kleines Mädchen gefangen hielten und mit diesem noch immer unter den Felsen begraben liegen.

Eine Sage aber ist zumindest in Ansätzen historisch belegt. Nachdem die Donau einige Kilometer hinter Spitz eine ihrer schönen Kehren gemacht und dabei Weinterrassen und Marillengärten gestreift hat, erreicht sie die Weinstadt Dürnstein. Über ihr, zwischen den düster bewaldeten Felsnadeln, liegt die gleichnamige Ruine. In ihr wurde um 1192, als sie noch stolze Ritterburg war, niemand Geringeres als der englische König Richard Löwenherz gefangen gehalten. Bei seiner Rückkehr vom Dritten Kreuzzug wurde Richard von Herzog Leo-

the setting of eerie legends and sagas. These tell of an Austrian Lorelei who lured ships on the Danube with her spellbinding singing and golden hair and made them crash into the rocks of the Wachau, or of the devil, who piled up rocky pinnacles, always for the purpose of hurting someone. One tale tells of dwarves that lived in the rocky caves and kept a little girl imprisoned there; people say they are still buried with her under the rocks today.

But one legend is at least partly based on historical events. A few kilometers beyond Spitz, after the Donau has made another of its lovely turns, passing terraced vineyards and apricot orchards as it goes, it arrives at the wine-growing town of Dürnstein. Above it, the ruins of Dürnstein Castle lie among dark, forested rocky pinnacles. Around 1192, when it was still a proud knight's castle, none other than the king of England, Richard the Lionhearted, was held prisoner here. As he returned

pold V. von Österreich gefangen genommen und später an seine politischen Gegner Kaiser Heinrich VI. und König Philipp August von Frankreich übergeben. Doch zuvor kerkerte Leopold den englichen König auf Burg Dürnstein ein. Der getreue Sänger Bondel soll jedoch auf der Suche nach seinem König gewesen sein. So zog er von Ort zu Ort und sang vor jeder Burg das Lieblingslied Richards – immer ohne Erfolg. Als er schließlich hoffnungslos vor den Fenstern von Dürnstein das Lied anstimmte, stimmte Richard in die zweite Strophe ein. Genützt hat das allerdings weder König noch Sänger: Richard wurde dem Kaiser überstellt und fortan auf Burg Trifels bei Speyer gefangen gehalten. Erst 1194 wurde er – nach Zahlung eines beträchtlichen Lösegelds durch seine Mutter, Eleonore von Aquitanien – wieder freigelassen.

Es dürfte vor allem diese Gefangenschaft Richard Löwenherz' sein, dessen Name unweigerlich mit dem Mythos um

from the Third Crusade, Richard was captured by Duke Leopold V of Austria and later handed over to his political opponents, Emperor Henry VI and King Philip II Augustus of France. Prior to that, however, Leopold incarcerated the English king in Dürnstein Castle. The faithful singer Blondel apparently went in search of his king. He went from place to place singing Richard's favorite song in front of every castle, always without success. But finally, when he started singing before the windows of Dürnstein, no longer hopeful, Richard joined him on the second verse. Sadly, his efforts benefited neither the king nor the singer: Richard was handed over to the emperor and from then on held prisoner in Trifels Castle near Speyer. He was only released in 1194 after his mother, Eleanor of Aquitaine, paid a large ransom.

The captivity of Richard the Lionhearted, whose name is inextricably linked with the legend of Robin Hood, is most

▲ Dürnstein sticht durch seinen blauen Kirchturm und die mächtige Burgruine aus all dem Sehenswerten an der Donau noch einmal hervor.
▲ Dürnstein is distinctive even among the many attractions along the Danube with its blue church tower and mighty castle ruins.

Robin Hood verbunden ist, die heute über 1,5 Millionen Touristen im Jahr anzieht, aber auch die grandiose Aussicht von den Wachaufelsen hinab auf das Donautal, das Waldviertel im Rücken der Ruine und den Dunkelsteinerwald am gegenüberliegenden Ufer.

Unterhalb der Ruine am Donaustrand liegt die Stadt Dürnstein, die von Weitem zunächst einmal durch den Turm der Stiftskirche hervorsticht – und zwar vor allem farblich. Sein leuchtendes Himmelblau ist einzigartig an der oberen Donau, an deren Ufern die Kirchen bisher vor allem in Gelbtönen erstrahlten. Die früher einmal gotische Anlage des Augustiner-Chorherrenstifts wurde im 18. Jahrhundert barockisiert, wobei auch der Kirchturm neu gestaltet und mit Reliefs zu den Leiden Christi überzogen wurde. Im Innern des heute als Begegnungsstätte genutzten Stifts ist der Besucher manchmal

likely what draws 1.5 million tourists to this spot each year. But the magnificent views from the Wachau cliffs down into the Danube Valley, the Waldviertel behind the ruins and the Dunkelstein Forest on the opposite bank also play a role.

Dürnstein lies beneath the castle ruins on the shores of the Danube, noticeable at first because of the tower of the monastic church–in all its bright color. Its luminous, sky-blue shade is unique on the Upper Danube, where most of the churches so far have been painted in bright shades of yellow. The formerly Gothic structure of this Augustinian abbey received an eighteenth-century baroque makeover, during which the church tower was newly designed and covered in reliefs depicting the suffering of Christ. The interior of the abbey, currently used as a community center, sometimes leaves visitors a little speechless, as the color scheme is rather flashy even by

ein wenig sprachlos, denn selbst für eine barocke Ausstattung ist die Farbgebung recht auffällig. Das gilt schon in der Marienkirche, vor allem aber am „Heiligen Grab" im Kreuzgang. Das übrige Dürnstein ist mit seinem Schloss, dem alten Klarissenkloster, den hübschen Gassen und lauschigen Lokalen der ideale Donautouristenort. Und hier sollte man unbedingt eine der weiteren Spezialitäten der Wachau probieren – die unvergleichlich saftigen Marillen, hier zu Knödeln, Strudel oder Brand verarbeitet. Wer nicht zur Marillenernte nach Dürnstein kommt, sollte die Stadt zur Blüte besuchen, wenn das Tal rundherum blassrosa leuchtet.

Die Donau macht eine letzte Kurve, dann öffnet sich das Tal: Rechts sieht man auf einem der letzten Wachaufelsen Kloster Göttweig, das zusammen mit Krems am linken Flussufer den Ausgang der Wachau markiert. Das Donautal wird breit und dicht besiedelt, das Flussbett der Donau zunehmend

baroque standards. This is already so in the Marienkirche, but is especially striking at the Holy Grave in the cloisters. The rest of Dürnstein–including the castle, the old St. Clare monastery, picturesque streets and inviting restaurants–makes for an ideal Danube tourist locale. It's the ideal place to try some of the additional Wachau specialties, such as the incomparably *Marillen* (juicy apricots) that are made into *Knödel* (dumplings), strudel and brandy. If you can't visit Dürnstein during the apricot harvest, the town is also spectacular when the trees are in bloom and the surrounding valley glitters in pale pink.

The Danube makes a final curve, and then the valley opens up. To the right, Göttweig Abbey is visible atop one of the last Wachau cliffs. Along with the town of Krems on the left bank, it marks the outlet of the Wachau Valley. The Danube Valley becomes wide and densely populated, and the riverbed becomes straighter. Forest alternates with meadows, nature

▾ Kloster Göttweig: Hier verlässt die Donau die Wachau.
▾ The Danube leaves the Wachau behind here at Göttweig Abbey.

gerader, Wald wechselt mit Wiesen, Naturparks mit Äckern ab. Schließlich erreicht die Donau Klosterneuburg und trennt sich dahinter – unterbrochen durch die schmale, aber gut 20 Kilometer lange Donauinsel – in zwei Arme. Rechts der Hauptstrom, links die Neue Donau, ein Entlastungsarm und gleichzeitig Naherholungsgebiet und Badeanstalt der Wiener. Denn kurz hinter Klosterneuburg fließt die Donau – schnurgerade und in Beton gegossen – in die österreichische Hauptstadt ein. Dort trennt sich am linken Ufer bald der Donaukanal – einst der Hauptarm des Flusses – ab, der die Bezirke Brigittenau und Leopoldstadt vom Wiener Zentrum trennt und sie als Insel zurücklässt. In Leopoldstadt liegt der viel besungene Prater mit seinen blühenden Bäumen, dem Riesenrad und dem Lusthaus, in dem sich zu Kaisers Zeiten Adel und Bürgertum vergnügten.

Das eigentliche Zentrum der früher größten und wichtigsten Stadt an der Donau liegt rechts des Donaukanals. Als im Zuge der Donauregulierung im 19. Jahrhundert das heutige Donaubett gegraben wurde, verlor Wien seinen direkten Kon-

preserves with farmland. The Danube finally reaches Klosterneuburg, and shortly thereafter splits into two branches separated by the narrow Danube Island, which is a good 20 km (12.5 miles) long. The main Danube River flows to the right of the island. The New Danube on the left diverts floodwaters away from Vienna, and also serves as a recreational area and swimming hole for the Viennese. For just beyond Klosterneuburg—straight as an arrow in its concrete bed—the Danube flows into the Austrian capital. The Danube Canal, once the river's main tributary, breaks away on the left bank. The canal separates Brigittenau and Leopoldstadt from center-city Vienna, making islands of the two districts. The much-touted Prater, the park where the aristocracy and bourgeoisie amused themselves in imperial times, boasting picturesque trees, a Ferris wheel and the Lusthaus café-restaurant, is located in Leopoldstadt.

The actual center of what was once the largest and most important city on the Danube lies to the right of the Danube Canal. When its current riverbed was dug during a phase of Danube "improvements" in the nineteenth century, Vienna lost

▾ Art Nouveau und ...
▾ Art nouveau and ...

▾ ... Graffitikunst treffen am Ufer des Donaukanals aufeinander.
▾ ... the art of graffiti are juxtaposed on the banks of the Danube Canal.

takt zum Fluss – doch das tut der Schönheit der Stadt keinen Abbruch. Bis zu deren Zerfall im Jahr 1918 war Wien das imperiale wie geistige und kulturelle Zentrum der Donaumonarchie, und das sieht man ihr an.

Jede Epoche hat ihre imposanten Bauwerke hinterlassen, Sinnbilder der kaiserlichen Macht, des städtischen und bürgerlichen Wohlstandes, der geistigen Eliten, Zeugnisse einer einzigartigen kulturellen, gesellschaftlichen Vielfalt. Das Wiener Bauwerk der Gotik ist der Stephansdom. Die gotische Neugestaltung des Doms geht auf das 14. Jahrhundert zurück, doch gab es romanische Vorgängerbauten, die im Westteil der Kirche noch erhalten sind. In seiner heutigen Gestalt ist der Stephansdom das Wahrzeichen, die Pummerin – die 21.383 Kilogramm schwere Glocke im Nordturm – die Stimme Österreichs. Die berühmten farbigen Ziegel des Daches aber sind im Zuge der Restaurierung unter Kaiser Franz I. verlegt worden: Der österreichische Reichsadler mit dem kaiserlichen Monogramm ziert die eine Seite, der Bundesadler mit falscher Kopfhaltung seit 1950 die andere Seite des Domdachs. Die

its direct connection to the river. But this doesn't detract from the city's beauty. Until the collapse of the Danube monarchy in 1918, Vienna was its imperial, spiritual and cultural center, as is still evident today.

Every epoch has left a legacy of imposing buildings, symbols of imperial power, of urban and bourgeois affluence, and of the intellectual elite, testaments to Vienna's unique cultural and social diversity. *The* Viennese example of Gothic architecture is the Stephansdom (St. Stephen's Cathedral). The Gothic reconfiguration of the cathedral dates back to the fourteenth century, but parts of an earlier Romanesque structure have been preserved in the western part of the church. In its present form, Stephansdom is the symbol of Austria, and its voice is Old Pummerin, a massive bell in the north tower that weighs 21,383 kg (over 47,000 pounds). The cathedral's famously colorful roof tiles were laid during the restoration made under Emperor Francis I: the Austrian imperial eagle with the imperial monogram decorate one side of the roof, while the federal eagle–its head positioned incorrectly since 1950–graces on the other

▾ Das kaiserliche Wappen auf dem Dach des Stephansdoms
▾ The imperial coat of arms on the roof of St. Stephen's Cathedral

▾ Der moderne Donauturm – Wahrzeichen eines neuen Wiens
▾ The modern Danube Tower, symbol of a new Vienna

▲ Otto Wagners Majolikahaus – eines der schönsten Jugendstilhäuser Wiens
▲ Otto Wagner's Majolica House, one the most beautiful Jugendstil buildings in Vienna

107 Meter lange Kathedrale besitzt vier Türme, von denen der Südturm mit 136,4 Metern nicht nur der höchste, sondern auch der einzige freistehende Turm ist.

Doch das eigentliche Gesicht der historischen Altstadt, von der UNESCO 2001 zum Weltkulturerbe ernannt, wird durch das Gemisch unterschiedlicher Stile geprägt: Die Hofburg, Residenz der österreichischen Kaiser, ist selbst ein Konglomerat unterschiedlicher Epochen – beispielsweise der Renaissance, des Barock, des Historismus und des Klassizismus. Dazu gehören auch die barocken Schlösser Belvedere und Schönbrunn, das historistische Palais Ferstel mit dem berühmten Kaffeehaus „Central", die gründerzeitlichen Wohnhäuser, Sinnbild

side. The cathedral is 107 meters (351 feet) long and has four towers. Standing 136.4 meters (447.5 feet) high, the south tower is not only the tallest, but also the only freestanding one.

But the true face of the Historic Center of Vienna, named a World Heritage Site by UNESCO in 2001, is one shaped by a unique mixture of varied styles. The Hofburg, residence of the Austrian emperors, is itself a conglomeration of different architectural periods, including Renaissance and baroque, historicism and classicism. Other examples are the baroque Belvedere and Schönbrunn Palaces, the historicist Palais Ferstel containing the famous Café Central, and elegant residences from the *Gründerzeit* (period of economic development after

eines erstarkenden Bürgertums, die in Wien ganze Straßenzüge füllen, und natürlich die sensationellen Jugendstilbauten. Unter ihnen gehören die Kirche am Steinhof und das Majolikahaus von Otto Wagner sowie die Secession mit Gustav Klimts „Beethovenfries" von Joseph Olbrich zu den Schönsten.

Bei so viel Prunk und Pracht sollten sich Besucher darauf besinnen, dass das eigentliche Herz der Stadt nicht in ihrer Architektur und anderen hochkarätigen Kulturschätzen liegt, sondern in den Kaffeehäusern. Mit einer Zeitung oder vielleicht auch einem Buch bei Mokka, Melange oder Einspänner, Buchteln oder Palatschinken im traditionellen Hawelka oder im Prückel mit seinem 1950er-Jahre-Charme zu sitzen gehört ebenso zum Wiener Alltag wie zu den Besonderheiten der Stadt.

1840), symbols of the burgeoning middle class that still fill entire city blocks in Vienna. Also integral are the sensational Jugendstil buildings, among which the Church of St. Leopold, Otto Wagner's Majolica House, and the Secession Hall by co-founder Joseph Olbrich with Gustav Klimt's *Beethoven Frieze* are exceptional.

In the midst of so much pomp and splendor, one shouldn't forget that the essence of Vienna lies not in its architecture or other outstanding cultural treasures, but in its cafés. To sit in the traditional Café Hawelka or the 1950s charm of Café Prückel with a newspaper or maybe even a book while enjoying any of the myriad Austrian coffee specialties with a *Buchtel* (yeast bun) or *Palatschinken* (Austrian-style crepe) is as much a part of everyday life in Vienna as it is a special feature of the city.

▼ Ein Traum in „Schönbrunner Gelb", eigentlich Goldocker: die kaiserliche Sommerresidenz Schönbrunn
▼ The dreamy Schönbrunn Palace, summer residence of emperors, is a distinctive yellow ochre color.

Wenn man das urbane Wien flussabwärts verlässt, ist die Ungarische Pforte, das auch Hainburger oder (in der Slowakei) Thebener Pforte genannte kleine Durchbruchtal an der Grenze zu Ungarn und der Slowakei, nicht mehr weit. Dort wird die Donau Österreich verlassen – allerdings nicht, bevor sie noch einmal mit der ganzen Fülle ihrer Natur prahlt. Direkt hinter Wien nämlich finden sich noch Donauauwälder, wie man sie so nah an einer Stadt, unmittelbar an einer Hauptverkehrswasserstraße, nicht erwarten würde. Es ist eine mystisch anmutende Landschaft, die sich dem Wanderer oder Bootsfahrer eröffnet. Altarme, sumpfige Wiesen, Inseln, Bannwälder ... Die Natur wird in dem zum Nationalpark ernannten Gebiet zu einem Großteil sich selbst überlassen.

Die Auwälder sind zu jeder Jahreszeit ein Erlebnis: Im Winter wirken sie wie eine karge, aber lichtdurchflutete Gegend, deren zugefrorene Teiche und dick mit Eiszapfen behängte Bäume und Sträucher recht unwirklich und bizarr erscheinen.

▼ In den Donauauen um Hainburg bestimmen Teiche, ...
▼ In the Danube floodplain around Hainburg, ponds, ...

Heading downriver from cosmopolitan Vienna, it isn't far to the Porta Hungarica, also called the Hainburger or (in Slovakia) Devín Gate, which is a natural gate in the Danube Valley at the border to Hungary and Slovakia. This is where the Danube leaves Austria, but not before she shows off her glorious natural wonders one last time. For just beyond Vienna there are still riverside forests on the Danube of a quality you wouldn't expect to find so close to a city or directly beside a major waterway. Hikers and boaters find themselves in a mystical landscape of oxbow lakes, swampy meadows, islands, protected forests and more. The area has been designated the Donau-Auen National Park, and for the most part, the natural world has been left to fend for itself.

The wetlands are an experience at any time of year. In winter the land is barren, yet flooded with light, and the frozen ponds surrounded by trees and bushes with numerous icicles hanging from them make a rather surrreal, bizarre impres-

▼ ... Feuchtwiesen, ...
▼ ... marshes, ...

▲ ... Altarme und ...
▲ ... oxbow lakes and ...

▲ ... dichte Wälder die Landschaft.
▲ ... dense woods dominate the landscape.

Mit dem Frühling aber bricht ein üppiges Leben im Nationalpark aus: Keine andere österreichische Landschaft kann einen größeren Artenreichtum aufweisen. Wilde Orchideen wachsen im Mai, Engelwurz, Klebriger Salbei und Aronstab im Sommer. Die Altarme, die von der vom Aussterben bedrohten Sumpfschildkröte bevölkert werden, sind von Seerose, Wasserschlauch, Schwertlilie und Wasserminze überwuchert. Darunter tummeln sich Welse, Grundeln und Hechte, Frösche leben an den Ufern, die wiederum von Purpurreihern, Graureihern und im Winter von Seeadlern vertilgt werden. Insgesamt sind es etwa 700 Pflanzen- und 5000 Tierarten, die in diesem Naturparadies zwischen Wien und Hainburg einen außergewöhnlichen Lebensraum finden.

Mit ihm verabschiedet sich die Donau von Österreich, gut 1000 Kilometer hat der Fluss seit Donaueschingen nun zurückgelegt. Eine kleine Weile noch ist die Donau Grenzfluss zur Slowakei, dann wird sie dort zur Dunaj.

sion. In springtime, everything comes abundantly to life in the national park. No other Austrian landscape boasts a greater diversity of flora and fauna. Wild orchids appear in May; angelica, Jupiter's sage and arum in the summer months. Oxbow lakes, populated with mud turtles threatened with extinction, are overgrown with water lilies, bladderwort, irises and water mint. Catfish, gobies and pike splash around beneath them, while frogs live in the shallow water around the edges. But frogs are also food for purple and gray herons, and for sea herons in the winter. In all, seven hundred species of plants and five thousand species of animals make their home in this exceptional habitat between Vienna and Hainburg.

As we leave Donau-Auen National Park, the Danube says farewell to Austria. The river has traveled a good thousand kilometers (620 miles) from its source in Donaueschingen. For a short while longer, the Danube constitutes the border with Slovakia, where it will become the Dunaj.

▲ Fünf Jahre, nachdem sie endlich unabhängig werden konnte, stiftete 1998 auch die Slowakei eine Tafel für den Quelltopf in Donaueschingen.
▲ Five years after independence was finally achieved, Slovakia also donated a plaque for the wellspring in Donaueschingen.

Die slowakisch-ungarische Donau

Wer mit dem Schiff von Österreich kommend in die Slowakei einreist, scheint vordergründig nichts Neues zu entdecken: Unmittelbar hinter einer Donaukehre mündet die March – auch sie Grenzfluss zwischen Österreich und der Slowakei – in die Donau, und dort überragt eine weitere Burgruine, Devin, den Fluss. Doch der Schein trügt: Es ist das Tor zum Osten, das man nun durchfährt. Die Ausläufer der Ostalpen treffen auf die Kleinen Karpaten. Einst trafen hier Salz- und Bernsteinstraße aufeinander. Und die Burgruine Devin selbst ist auch nicht etwa nur der ehemalige Sitz eines Donauraubritters: Für die Slowaken ist sie die Keimzelle der slawischen Nationen.

Der Ort war bereits in der Jungsteinzeit besiedelt und der Felsvorsprung zu römischen Zeiten ein wichtiger strategischer

The Slovakian-Hungarian Danube

Someone traveling from Austria to Slovakia by boat may not notice anything new at first. Immediately after a bend in the Danube, the Morava River flows into the Danube to form part of the river border between Austria and Slovakia. And it is at this point that the ruins of yet another castle, the Devin, tower over the river. But appearances can be deceiving, for you are now traveling through the gate to Eastern Europe. The foothills of the Eastern Alps meet the Little Carpathians, and salt and amber trade routes used to cross here. The ruins of the Devin Castle are not only the former seat of a Danube robber baron, but for Slovaks, also the birthplace of the Slavic nations.

This place was already settled in the Neolithic age, and in Roman times the rocky ledge was an important strategic point that secured the border of the Roman Empire. The

▲ Hrad Devin, Burg Devin, bewacht den Eingang zur Porta Hungarica bzw. zur Slowakei.
▲ Devin Castle guards the entrance to the Porta Hungarica and to Slovakia.

Punkt, der die Grenze des Imperium Romanum sicherte. Nachdem die Burg ab dem 9. Jahrhundert errichtet und in den späteren Jahrhunderten mehr und mehr zur Festung ausgebaut worden war, trotzte sie allen Eroberungsversuchen – bis die Truppen Napoleons sie 1809 einnahmen und sprengten. Vom Wasser aus fällt insbesondere der kleine, durch eine Mauer mit der Burg verbundene Jungfernturm unmittelbar über dem Donaustrand ins Auge: Hier stürzte sich der Sage nach eine junge Braut in ihrer Hochzeitsnacht in die Donaufluten, nachdem ihr Gatte vor ihren Augen ermordet worden war.

172 Flusskilometer der Donau – slowakisch Dunaj – gehören zur Slowakei, von denen allerdings insgesamt 150 als Grenze zu Österreich bzw. Ungarn fungieren. Lediglich auf dem Gebiet um die slowakische Hauptstadt Bratislava erstreckt sich der Staat beidseits des Flusses. Als die Slowakei im Jahre 1993 ihre Unabhängigkeit erlangte, wurde Bratislava,

castle was first erected in the ninth century, and in later centuries was converted into an increasingly impregnable fortress. Until Napoleon's troops captured and destroyed it in 1809, the stronghold resisted all attempts to conquer it. Seen from the river, the small Maiden's Tower just above the Danube grabs your attention; a wall connects the tower to the castle. According to legend, it was here that a young bride plunged into the waters of the Danube after her husband was murdered before her eyes on their wedding night.

The Danube, or Dunaj in Slovak, flows through Slovakia for 172 km (107 miles). For 150 of these kilometers (93 miles), the river serves as the border between Slovakia and Austria or Hungary. Only in the area around the capital, Bratislava, does the city span both sides of the river. When Slovakia gained its independence in 1993, Bratislava

▲ Bratislava: Einst Hauptstadt des Großmährischen Reichs, dann Ungarns, ist sie heute Hauptstadt der Slowaken.
▲ Once the capital of the Greater Moravian Empire and then of Hungary, Bratislava is now the capital of Slovakia.

im Deutschen auch unter dem Namen Preßburg bekannt, zur Hauptstadt ernannt. Die junge Hauptstadt, die vom Donauufer von einer imposant-trutzigen Burganlage dominiert wird, erinnert an das nicht ferne Wien und unterscheidet sich doch deutlich von ihm.

Ähnlich ist Bratislava der österreichischen Hauptstadt etwa in seiner Kaffeehaustradition – auch hier ein Relikt von Türkenbelagerung und k. u. k. Monarchie. Und wie zu Zeiten Letzterer herrscht noch immer ein starker kultureller Austausch mit Wien. Doch das Erscheinungsbild Bratislavas ist ein ganz anderes. Zwar gibt es – weil die Ungarn im 16. bis 18. Jahrhundert ihre Residenz von Buda hierher verlegten – die typischen barocken habsburgischen Palais; doch der Prunk Wiens wich einer schlichteren Eleganz, die sich vor allem hinter geschnitzten hölzernen Toren versteckt und in ihrer ganzen Schönheit in den freundlichen Innenhöfen entfaltet – die hier wie in Wien Pawlatschen genannt werden. Andere Stra-

(also known by its German name, Pressburg) was chosen as the capital. An imposing, defiant castle complex on the shore of the Danube dominates the cityscape of the young capital, which is reminiscent of Vienna, yet also clearly differs from it.

Bratislava's coffeehouse tradition is similar to that of the Austrian capital, and here, too, it is a relic of Turkish sieges and the Dual Monarchy. As in the era of Dual Monarchy, Bratislava still has very strong cultural ties with Vienna. But Bratislava has an entirely different appearance. Since Hungary moved its royal seat from Buda to Bratislava from the sixteenth to eighteenth centuries, one does find typical baroque Habsburg palaces here. But in Bratislava, the grandiosity of Vienna gave way to a simpler elegance that is mainly hidden behind carved wooden gates and only unfolds its full beauty within welcoming interior courtyards. Here and in Vienna, these courtyards are called *Pawlatschen*. Other residential

▲ Stolze barocke Bürgerhäuser säumen die Straßen Bratislavas.
▲ Proud baroque town houses line the streets of Bratislava.

ßenzüge der Altstadt, die sich rund um den gotischen Martinsdom, in dem unter anderem Maria Theresia gekrönt wurde, erstreckt, muten beinahe dörflich an. Ihre zweistöckigen Bürgerhäuser werden seit der Unabhängigkeit und dem Beitritt der Slowakei zur EU aufwendig restauriert, und so wird die seit dem Zweiten Weltkrieg touristisch so vernachlässigte Stadt mehr und mehr zum Touristenmagneten.

Die Donau wird in der slowakischen Metropole, die bis ins 19. Jahrhundert kaum von Slowaken, sondern in der Mehrheit von Österreichern, Ungarn und Deutschen bewohnt war, von der Neuen Brücke (offiziell: Brücke des slowakischen Volksaufstands) überspannt. Sie wurde 1972 als erste europäische Schrägseilbrücke errichtet und ist auf ihrem Pylon mit einem UFO-förmigen Restaurant bekrönt. Der Besuch lohnt, denn von hier aus kann man an klaren Tagen bis nach Österreich und über die Ungarische Tiefebene – die hier entlang des Flusses verläuft – schauen. Kurz hinter Bratislava erweitert sich

streets in Old Bratislava that stretch around the Gothic St. Martin's Cathedral—where Maria Theresa, among others, was crowned—could almost be in a village. Since Slovakia became independent and joined the European Union (EU), the two-story town houses have been painstakingly restored. The city that was so neglected as a tourist destination after World War II is increasingly becoming a magnet for visitors.

The New Bridge, officially named the Bridge of Slovak National Uprising, spans the Danube in a metropolis that had very few Slovak residents until the nineteenth century; prior to that, most of the inhabitants were Austrians, Hungarians and Germans. The bridge was built in 1972 and was the first asymmetrical cable-stayed bridge in Europe. The UFO-shaped restaurant that rests on its pylon is well worth visiting, since on clear days it offers a view extending all the way to Austria and over the Little Hungarian Plain alongside the river. A short distance beyond Bratislava, the Danube Basin widens almost

▲ Pappeln, Schilf und nur kleine Staustufen – so präsentiert sich die Kleine Donau jenseits der Großen Schütt.
▲ Poplars, reeds and only very small barrages—these are typical of the Little Danube on the far side of Great Rye Island.

das Donaubecken fast seenartig. Am linken Donauufer zweigt die Kleine Donau ab, schlängelt sich in zahllosen Mäandern durch die Ebene und mündet bei dem slowakischen Örtchen Komarno in den Waag, der zurück in die Donau fließt. So entsteht eine 1540 Quadratkilometer große Insel, die größte Flussinsel Europas, die sich Große Schüttinsel bzw. Zitny ostrov nennt. Sie ist durch ihr warmes Klima und die vielen Nebenarme und Wasserläufe rund um Donau, Kleine Donau und Waag die fruchtbarste Region der Slowakei. Dort hat sich eine ursprüngliche Landschaft erhalten, die mit Sümpfen, dichten Schilfgürteln, Teichen, Feuchtweiden und Pappelwäldern sowie einer artenreichen Tierwelt verschiedene regionale Naturschutzgebiete bildet. Es ist ein Bild voller Romantik, zu dem auch solch historische Wassermühlen wie die von Jelka oder die Schiffsmühle in Kolarovo beitragen, an denen man bei einer Bootstour vorbeikommt. Auch die überdachte Holzbrücke von Kolarovo, die über die Kleine Donau führt, ist mit

like a lake. The Little Danube branches off the left side of the Danube and meanders its way through the plain in countless bends to the Slovakian village of Komarno, where it flows into the Vag (or Vah) River, which then flows back into the Danube. This creates Europe's largest river island, encompassing about 1,540 square km (595 square miles). It is called Great Rye Island in English, and Zitny Ostrov in Slovak. Thanks to its warm climate and the numerous tributaries and waterways around the Danube, Little Danube and Vag rivers, the island is Slovakia's most fertile region. A pristine landscape has survived here that includes various regional conservation areas with swamps, thick reed zones, ponds, marshes and poplar forests, as well as a rich variety of fauna. It paints a highly romantic picture. Historic water mills such as the one at Jelka or the ship mill in Kolarovo, which boat tours pass by, only enhance the impression. The covered wooden bridge in Kolarovo passes over the Little Danube, and at 86 meters (282 feet), it is the

86 Meter Länge die längste ihrer Art in Europa. Auch am rechten Ufer der Hauptdonau zweigt kurz hinter Bratislava ein Nebenarm ab, die Mosoni Duna. Sie liegt bereits auf ungarischem Staatsgebiet, und von nun an bleibt die Donau, Dunaj oder ungarisch Duna der Grenzfluss zwischen den Staaten. Das Gebiet nennt sich Kleine Schütt und bildet ebenfalls viele Altarme und Seitenarme mit herrlichen Auwäldern.

Dass Große und Kleine Schütt, die aus dem von der Donau mitgeführten Geröll und Schlamm entstanden sind, heute noch diese außergewöhnlich intakte Flora und Faune aufweisen, ist vor allem der Weitsicht der ungarischen Regierung zu verdanken. Hatten Ungarn und die damalige Tschechoslowakei im Jahr 1977 noch die Aufstauung der Donau zur Energiegewinnung in diesem Abschnitt beschlossen, so kündigte Ungarn 1990 den Vertrag: Zu groß wäre der ökologische Schaden gewesen. Und so wurde nur das Kraftwerk von Gabcikovo realisiert, an dem Schiffsreisende vorbeikommen.

longest of its kind in Europe. Shortly after Bratislava, a tributary branches off from the right bank of the main Danube, the Mosoni-Duna. This tributary is already on Hungarian land, and from here onward the Danube, Dunaj, or Duna (in Hungarian) constitutes the border between the two countries. Called Little Rye, the area has many oxbow lakes and river branches with beautiful riparian woods.

Great Rye and Little Rye were originally created from debris and mud carried along by the Danube. Largely due to the foresight of the Hungarian government, their flora and fauna are still unusually intact. In 1977 Hungary and the former Czechoslovakia had agreed to dam this section of the Danube for energy production, but Hungary cancelled the contract in 1990, because the ecological damage would have been too great. Instead, only the Gabcikovo power station was completed, and people traveling by ship pass it.

▾ Historische Wassermühlen, wie die bei Jelka, überraschen immer wieder an den Gewässern der Zitny ostrov.
▾ Along the waterways surrounding Great Rye Island, historic water mills such as this one near Jelka will surprise you time and again.

Kaum ein Volk ist so sehr mit der Donau verbunden wie die Ungarn. Naturschutzgebiete säumen ihre Ufer, und für die Budapester sind die Strände der Donau ein Naherholungsgebiet, an dem man ganze Tage verbringen kann, den Fluss, sein Leben und seine Ruhe beobachtend und die eigene Vergänglichkeit bedenkend.

„In Donauwellen sah ich Heutiges, Einstiges, Künftiges Vergehen ...", schrieb einer der bedeutendsten ungarischen Lyriker, Attila Joszef, in seinem Gedicht „An der Donau". Man liest Auszüge daraus auf einer der beiden ungarischen Tafeln am Donaueschinger Quelltopf. Und auch für Peter Esterhazy, ungarischer Schriftsteller und Essayist, birgt die Donau das ungarische Leben: „Ich begriff, dass ich von diesem Fluss alles bekommen würde. Auskunft über die Berge und Wasser, Geschichte, Volkskunde, Gegenwart, Zukunft, Hochwasser und

Hardly anyone is so closely connected to the Danube as the people of Hungary. Nature preserves line its banks, and for the residents of Budapest, the Danube beaches are a nearby recreational area where you can spend entire days observing the river, its life, its peacefulness and even pondering your own impermanence.

"In the Danube's waves I saw the present, the past and the future..." wrote one of Hungary's most important poets, Attila Jozsef, in *By the Danube*. An excerpt from the poem is on one of the two Hungarian plaques at the river's source in Donaueschingen. For Hungarian writer and essayist Peter Esterhazy, as well, the Danube is the essence of Hungarian life: "I understood that I would get everything from this river. Information about the mountains and water, history, folklore, the present, future, high tides and droughts, swirling currents and fish

▾ Bereits in Donaueschingen zeigen die Ungarn, wie teuer ihnen der Strom ist.
▾ A plaque at the its source in Donaueschingen already testifies to the Hungarians' tremendous affection for the river.

Dürre, Stromwirbel und Fischsuppe und Menschen würden sein ...", liest man in „Donau abwärts".

Auf Zeitzeugen ungarischer Geschichte trifft man an der Duna, wie der Fluss in Ungarn heißt, überall, doch keiner hat für die Nation eine solche Bedeutung wie Esztergom, die Stadt, an der der Gran (ungarisch Hron) auf slowakischer Seite in die Donau mündet. Der Hügel an der Donau, der von der ehemaligen Hauptstadt Ungarns umgeben ist, ist nahezu ein nationales Heiligtum. Hier ließ Fürst Geza im Jahr 972 seine Residenz erbauen, deren Ruinen man wieder durchstreifen kann. Sein Sohn wurde hier geboren und am 17. August 1000 zu König Stephan I. von Ungarn gekrönt. Der erste König Ungarns ist heute der Nationalheilige des Landes, die nach ihm benannte Stephanskrone, Sinnbild der Einheit Ungarns, ziert noch immer das ungarische Wappen.

soup and people ..." he wrote in his novel *The Glance of Countess Hahn-Hahn (Down the Danube).*

There are numerous testaments to Hungarian history all along the Duna, as the river is called in Hungarian. But none has as much significance to the nation as Esztergom, the city where the Hron River flows into the Danube on the Slovak side. The hill on the Danube is surrounded by the former capital of Hungary and is virtually a national shrine. Prince Geza had his residence built here in 972, and you can wander through its ruins. His son was born here and on August 17, 1000, was crowned King Stephan I of Hungary. The first Hungarian king is now the country's patron saint. The Holy Crown of Hungary, symbolic of Hungarian unity, is named after him (Crown of St. Stephen) and still adorns the Hungarian coat of arms.

▾ Esztergom gilt mit seiner Kathedrale und den Ruinen der einstigen Residenz als ein Nationalheiligtum der Ungarn.
▾ With its cathedral and the ruins of the former royal residence, Esztergom is something like a Hungarian national shrine.

Neben den Ruinen der königlichen Residenz und von der Donau aus nicht zu übersehen liegt die Basilika von Esztergom, Maria Himmelfahrt. Auch wenn sich in gleicher Lage schon im Mittelalter eine Kirche befand, wurde der heutige Sitz des ungarisch-katholischen Erzbischofs erst im Jahr 1856 geweiht – acht Jahre, nachdem die ungarische Revolution blutig niedergeschlagen worden war. Die Kathedrale ist die größte katholische Kirche des Landes und den Ungarn ein Symbol für ihre Erhebung gegen die Habsburger Fremdherrschaft, auch wenn bei ihrer Weihe – die Franz Liszt mit seiner Graner Messe begleitete – Kaiser Franz Joseph I. anwesend war.

Kurz hinter Esztergom verlässt die Donau die Slowakei endgültig, und der Fluss ändert mit einem Mal seine Fließrichtung. Am sogenannten Donauknie macht bei der Stadt Vac die Donau einen fast rechtwinkligen Knick und fließt bei-

From the Danube, the Esztergom Basilica (dedicated to the Blessed Virgin Mary) next to the ruins of the royal residence can't be overlooked. Although there was a church on this very spot in the Middle Ages, the current seat of the Catholic Church in Hungary was not consecrated until 1856, just eight years after the Hungarian Revolution was put down with great bloodshed. The cathedral is the largest Catholic church in the country. Even though Emperor Francis Joseph I was present at its consecration—Franz Liszt accompanied the service with his Missa Solemnis—Hungarians still consider it a symbol of their uprising against Habsburg rule.

Shortly after Esztergom, the Danube leaves Slovakia for the last time, and the river suddenly changes direction from its previous east-west course. At the "Danube knee" near the town of Vac, the river practically bends at a right

▾ Kurz hinter Esztergom beginnt das Donauknie.
▾ The Danube Knee begins shortly after Esztergom.

nahe 400 Flusskilometer lang bis nach Kroatien nicht mehr in West-Ost-, sondern in Nord-Süd-Richtung. Dabei muss sie sich zunächst einmal – vorbei an der Stadt Visegrad mit den Ruinen ihres Renaissancepalastes – den Weg durch die Visegrader Berge bahnen, wobei sie sich in einen Haupt- und einen Nebenarm verzweigt und dazwischen die Insel Szentendre zurücklässt. Das gleichnamige Städtchen liegt am Westufer des Nebenarms und bildet mit seinen bunten Häuschen und der fruchtbaren Insel ein sehr beliebtes Ausflugsziel – vor allem bei den Budapestern.

Die Duna fließt nun die wenigen Kilometer bis zur ungarischen Hauptstadt durch ihr fruchtbares Schwemmland, dessen Äcker und Wiesen die Landschaft prägen. Direkt am Flussufer ist das Land dicht besiedelt – ein Zustand, der für das Ungarn der berühmten weiten Puszta nicht unbedingt ty-

angle and flows for the next 400 km (250 miles), all the way to Croatia, in a north-south direction. But she must first make her way past Visegrad and the ruins of its Renaissance palace and then through the Visegrad Mountains. The river splits into a main stream and a distributary, leaving behind Szentendre Island in the process. A little town by the same name lies on the west bank of the distributary. The town's colorful little houses and the lush island are a popular destination for outings, particularly among residents of Budapest.

The Duna now flows the few kilometers to the Hungarian capital through the fertile alluvial plain, and the landscape is covered with farmland and meadows. The land directly adjacent to the river is densely populated, a situation that is not typical of the wide Puszta (plains) for which Hungary is

▾ In zwei Armen frisst sich die Donau am Donauknie durch die Visegrader Berge und schließt dabei die schöne Insel Szentendre ein.
▾ Two branches of the Danube carve into the Visegrad Mountains at the Danube Knee, encircling beautiful Szentendre Island.

▲ Sie ist unbestritten die „Donauperle“: die ungarische Hauptstadt Budapest
▲ Budapest, capital of Hungary, is the undisputed "Pearl of the Danube."

pisch ist. Fährt man dagegen nur ein paar Kilometer ins Hinterland, erscheint das ungarische Leben wie das eines anderen Jahrhunderts: Pferd und Wagen, Hühner im Hof und kleine Äcker und Gärten, die den Bedarf dessen, was in der Küche gebraucht wird, decken, sind überall anzutreffen. Von der nahen Großstadt ist wenig zu spüren.

Die Donau erreicht unterdessen Budapest. Es ist nicht übertrieben, Ungarns Hauptstadt als die schönste Stadt entlang des Flusses zu bezeichnen. Sie ist – anders als Wien – eine echte Donaumetropole, die den Fluss in ihr tägliches Leben einbindet. Ihre Brücken – die älteste und berühmteste ist die filigrane Kettenbrücke – verbinden den rechten Stadtteil Buda mit Pest am linken Ufer. Majestätisch thront die Burg auf dem Budaer Burgberg, darunter erstreckt sich das malerische Burgviertel mit seinen engen Gassen. Von hier oben zeigt sich die Hauptstadt in all ihrer Pracht. Zur Linken liegen Fischerbastei und die Matthiaskirche, in der Kaiser Franz Josef I. und Prinzessin Elisabeth (Sissi) heirateten. Ein Blickfang ist auch das Parla-

famous. But if you travel just a short way into the backcountry, life in Hungary seems to belong to an earlier century: there are horses and wagons everywhere, chickens in the yards, small plots and gardens that provide whatever is needed for the food being prepared in the kitchens. There are few traces of the large city nearby.

Meanwhile, the Danube reaches Budapest. It is no exaggeration to say that the Hungarian capital is the most beautiful city along the Danube. Unlike Vienna, she is a true Danube metropolis, where the river is integrated into everyday life. Budapest bridges, the oldest and most famous of which is the sophisticated Chain Bridge, connect the city of Buda on the right bank with Pest on the left bank. Buda Castle majestically crowns Castle Hill, and the picturesque Buda Castle quarter with its narrow lanes stretches out beneath it. The capital can be seen in all its splendor from up here. To the left are the Fisherman's Bastion and St. Matthew's Cathedral, where Emperor Francis Joseph and Princess Elisabeth of Bavaria ("Sissi") were

ment am Pester Donauufer, dessen Bau von 1885 sich an der englischen Gotik orientiert. Dazwischen, mitten in der Donau, liegt die idyllische Margareteninsel, wohin König Bela IV. seine Tochter Margarete 1252 einem Gelübte gemäß als Nonne ins Kloster der Dominikanerinnen schickte. Der König wollte seine Tochter „opfern", sollte er im Krieg gegen die Tartaren, die sein Land zu jener Zeit bedrängten, siegen. Margarete starb noch nicht mal dreißigjährig im Kloster; sie wurde 1943 heiliggesprochen. Auf Pester Seite zweigt mitten in der Stadt ein Seitenarm der Donau ab; er wird erst im Süden, weit hinter der Stadt, wieder auf den Hauptarm treffen. Von den Budaer Hügeln aus lässt sich über die Donau und das flache Pest hinweg bis in die Große Ungarische Tiefebene hineinblicken. Dort schließt sich fruchtbares Ackerland direkt an Budapest an. Eine ländliche Idylle, der die hauptstädtische allerdings in nichts nachsteht.

Auf architektonische Highlights – vor allem der Gründerzeit und des Jugendstils – stößt der Besucher in Budapest beinahe überall. Das „Goldene Zeitalter" zwischen 1867 und 1914,

married. On the Pest side of the Danube, the Parliament Building, built in 1885 based on English Gothic architecture, catches the eye. In between the two lies the idyllic Margaret Island, right in the middle of the Danube. In the thirteenth century, King Bela IV had his daughter, Margaret, take religious vows in the Dominican nunnery there. The king wanted to "offer up" his daughter in exchange for his victory over the Tartars. Margaret died in the convent in 1270 before her thirtieth birthday, was beatified in 1789 and canonized in 1934. In the middle of the city, a side arm of the Danube branches off the Pest side and only rejoins the main stream far below Budapest. The Buda Hills are the perfect vantage point for a view over the Danube and the flat city of Pest to the Great Hungarian Plain that stretches out beyond it. The fertile farmland of Hungary's granary borders directly on Budapest, a pastoral idyll that is every bit as wonderful as the capital "environment."

Visitors to Budapest will find architectural marvels, particularly those of the Gründerzeit and Jugendstil, at every turn. The

das auch für die Pracht Wiens verantwortlich zeichnet, hat in Budapest nicht nur herrliche Bürgerhäuser, sondern auch den Prachtboulevard Andrassy ut mit der grandiosen Staatsoper hervorgebracht. Zu den beeindruckendsten Jugendstilbauten zählen Ödön Lechners Musikakademie, die Elisabethkirche, das Kunstgewerbemuseum mit seiner großartigen Eingangshalle und der Zoo, dessen Elefantenhaus allein schon sprachlos macht.

Es ist erstaunlich, wie abwechslungsreich Budapest bereits architektonisch ist: weltstädtisch das gründer- bis neuzeitliche Pest, fast dörflich das Viertel um den Burgberg mit seinen bunten Renaissance- und Barockhäusern. Der Burgberg selbst überragt trutzig die Stadt, und auf Pester Seite findet sich ein fast intaktes jüdisches Viertel, das sich nach dem Zweiten Weltkrieg erst langsam wieder mit jüdischer Kultur füllte und dessen prächtige, im maurisch-byzantinischen Stil errichtete

"Golden Age" between 1876 and 1914, which is also responsible for the splendor of Vienna, gave rise not only to the elegant town houses of Budapest, but also to the stately Andrassy Avenue, with its magnificent Hungarian State Opera House. Among the most impressive Jugendstil buildings are Ödön Lechner's Academy of Music, the Church of St. Elizabeth, the Arts and Crafts Museum with its gorgeous entrance hall and the Budapest Zoo, where the Elephant House alone can take your breath away.

The rich architectural variety of Budapest is truly astounding. Styles in cosmopolitan Pest range from *Gründerzeit* to the modern, while the colorful Renaissance and baroque houses around Castle Hill almost have the feel of a village. Castle Hill itself towers defiantly over the city. The Jewish Quarter in Pest is almost intact, but Jewish culture has only gradually returned to the city since World War II. The magnificent Great Synagogue, built in Moorish-Byzantine style, can accommodate

▾ Beinahe dörflich muten die Gassen im Budaer Burgviertel an.
▾ The lanes around Buda Castle have some of the atmosphere of a village.

▲ Mit knapper Not entging die im maurischen Stil errichtete Große Synagoge von Pest den Zerstörungen durch die Nazis.
▲ Built in Moorish style, the Great Synagogue of Pest just barely escaped destruction by the Nazis.

▲ Der international bedeutende Hafen der Donaumetropole Budapest birgt eine ganz eigene Faszination.
▲ The internationally significant harbor in the metropolis on the Donau is fascinating in its own way.

Synagoge 4000 Gläubige fasst. Im Haus daneben kam Theodor Herzl, Initiator des politischen Zionismus, zur Welt.

Nicht minder vielfältig ist das Leben in der Hauptstadt, das von den zahllosen Besatzern der Stadt mitgeprägt wurde. Relikte aus der Zeit der osmanischen Herrschaft sind die Bäder wie die Kaffeehäuser. Erstere nutzen die Quellen, die unterhalb von Burg- und Gellertberg aus der Erde sprudeln und die schon zu Zeiten der Römer und im Mittelalter bekannt waren, aber vor allem unter türkischer Fremdherrschaft zu herrlichen Bädern ausgebaut wurden. Erhalten davon ist unter anderem noch das Kaiserbad, doch wesentlich populärer und durch seinen leichten Jugendstilbau besonders eindrucksvoll ist das Gellertbad. Auch für die Kaffeehaustradition zeichnen die Türken letztendlich verantwortlich, brachten sie die schwarzen Bohnen doch mit an die Donau. Aber die Habsburger etablierten wie in Wien auch in der ungarischen Stadt die Kaffeehaustradition. Eines der berühmtesten Kaffeehäuser in Budapest ist das Café Gerbeaud, das 1858 eröffnet

4,000 worshippers. The founder of modern-day political Zionism, Theodor Herzl, was born in the house next door.

Life in the capital, having been shaped by countless occupiers over the centuries, is no less diverse. Remnants of Ottoman rule are the coffeehouses and the baths, which utilize the springs that bubble up from the earth beneath Castle Hill and Gellert Hill. The springs were already famous in Roman times and the Middle Ages, but were developed into the most marvelous baths under Turkish rule. The Lukács Baths are among those that have been preserved, but with its impressive, whimsical Jugendstil architecture, the Gellert Baths are much more popular. The Turks were also responsible for the coffeehouse tradition, as they brought the precious black beans with them as they traveled the Danube. As in Vienna, the Habsburgs established the coffeehouse tradition in this Hungarian city. One of the most famous coffeehouses in Budapest is Café Gerbeaud, which opened in 1858. As everywhere in the city, Dobos Torte (a seven-layer cake)

▲ Rackeve an der Kleinen Donau – für viele Ungarn ein Ort der Erholung
▲ Rackeve on the Little Danube is a place many Hungarians go to relax.

wurde. Wie überall in der Stadt sind auch hier Dobostorte und Esterhazy-Torte die Spezialitäten.

Budapest aber hat auch ein ganz anderes Gesicht: Rund um die Hauptstadt tummeln sich die typischen grauen sozialistischen Plattenbauten. Sie bieten vielfach den einzig bezahlbaren Wohnraum in der Metropole und werden mittlerweile häufig zu Niedrigenergiehäusern umgebaut, um dem modernen Wohnstandard zu entsprechen. Und – wie es sich für eine Großstadt an einer viel befahrenen Wasserstraße gehört – fehlt auch in Budapest nicht der international bedeutende Fracht- und Personenhafen.

Fährt man die Kleine Donau – das ist der in Budapest abzweigende Nebenarm – flussabwärts, eröffnet sich rund um das Städtchen Rackeve ein neues Urlaubsdomizil der Ungarn, vor allem der Budapester: Angler, Badende und Wassersportler aller Art nutzen die ländliche Ruhe, die nicht wie am Hauptstrom vom Schiffsverkehr belastet wird.

and Ersterhazy Torte, a multi-layered, chocolate buttercream pastry, are the specialties served here.

But there is also another very different side of Budapest. Typical, gray, Soviet-era prefabricated concrete slab buildings crowd around the perimeter of the capital; they frequently offer the only affordable living space in the metropolis. Many have been converted to low-energy housing in order to meet modern-day living standards. Budapest also has an international harbor for freighters and cruise ships, as would be expected of a major city on a much-traveled waterway.

Sailing downriver on the Little Danube, a distributary that branches off in Budapest, you'll encounter a new vacation spot around the village of Rackeve that is popular with Hungarians, especially residents of Budapest. Anglers, bathers and fans of water sports of all kinds enjoy the rural tranquility, a sharp contrast to the shipping traffic on the main river.

Auch auf der Hauptdonau wird es, je weiter es in den Süden Ungarns geht, wieder ländlicher – trotz der großen Schubverbände, die ihre tonnenschweren Lasten auf der Donau transportieren. Auwälder bestimmen wieder hin und wieder die Landschaft, zunächst wird das fruchtbare Donauschwemmland aber für die intensive Landwirtschaft genutzt. Angebaut wird unter anderem auch der berühmte rote scharfe Paprika. Es ist ein äußerst reicher Boden, der sich zwischen Donau und der weiter im Osten parallel zur Donau verlaufenden Theiß erstreckt, und neben Szeged in Ostungarn gilt Kalocsa an der Donau als eines der Paprikazentren des Landes. Die Häuser sind hier mit den roten Schoten behängt, und ein Paprikamuseum zeigt die Verarbeitung des scharfen Gewürzes, das in Schoten und als Pulver in die hiesige schmackhafte Fischsuppe kommt.

Doch nicht nur der Paprika gedeiht hier, auch die Tierwelt findet zwischen Theiß und Donau einen wichtigen Lebensraum. Störche bauen seit Jahrhunderten ihre Nester auf den Schornsteinen der Dörfer, und seit Neuestem wird der vom

As you travel farther south, the landscape becomes more rural again, even on the main portion of the Danube and despite the large barge trains that transport heavy loads of cargo along this route. Riverside forests will again determine the landscape from time to time, although initially, the fertile Danube alluvial plain is intensively farmed. The famous spicy red peppers ground to make paprika are among the crops grown here. The soil is extremely rich in the area between the Danube and the Tisza River, which runs parallel to the Danube to the east, and along with Szeged in southeastern Hungary, Kalocsa on the Danube is a center of Hungarian paprika production. Red peppers hang from the rafters of houses here, and a museum devoted to peppers shows how they process the spicy fruit that ends up, both whole and powdered, in the delicious fish soup that's a local specialty.

Peppers are not the only things that thrive here: the animal world also finds an important habitat between the Tisza and Danube. Storks have built their nests atop village chimneys for centuries, and endangered water buffaloes have

Störche kann man überall an der ungarischen Donau beobachten, ...
Storks can be seen all along the Hungarian Danube, ...

... Wasserbüffel weit weniger. Sie werden hier wieder angesiedelt und gezüchtet.
...but far fewer water buffaloes. They are being bred and reestablished here.

Aussterben bedrohte Wasserbüffel hier wieder angesiedelt. Im Süden des Landes taucht die Donau wieder in Auwälder ab: Der Gemencer Wald ist der größte Auwald Europas und gilt als einer der fischreichsten. Doch gefischt werden darf nur auf dem Hauptstrom, die verzweigten Seitenarme stehen unter Naturschutz.

Bevor die Donau die Grenze erreicht, fließt sie noch an der Stadt Mohacs vorbei. Sie sollte man vor allem zur Fastnachtszeit besuchen, wenn die Einwohner der Stadt sechs Tage in ihren aufwendigen Kostümen feiern. Aus Schafsfellen werden die Kostüme geschneidert, die Tiermasken in Handarbeit aus Holz geschnitzt. Mit Widderhörnern und Glocken ausstaffiert, geben sie ein erschreckend-schönes Bild ab. Wenige Kilometer hinter der Stadt erreicht die Donau – in Auwäldern versteckt – die ungarisch-kroatische Landesgrenze, um wenig später erneut zu einem Grenzfluss zu werden: dem zwischen Kroatien und Serbien.

recently been reestablished here. The Danube goes underground again in the riverside forests of southern Hungary. The Gemenc Forest is the largest tidal wood in Europe and has one of the richest supplies of fish. But fishing is only allowed in the main portion of the Danube, while the river's branches are protected by law.

Before reaching the border, the Danube must still flow past the town of Mohacs. The season leading up to Lent is the ideal time to visit Mohacs, when residents hold a six-day celebration in extravagant costumes. The costumes are made from sheepskin, and the wooden animal masks are hand-carved. Equipped with ram's horns and bells, they are shocking and beautiful at the same time. Just a few kilometers beyond Mohacs the Duna, still hidden among the woods, reaches the border of Hungary and Croatia. Shortly thereafter the river will once again become a border, this time between Croatia and Serbia.

▼ Bootstour durch den Gemencer Wald – ein romantisches Vergnügen
▼ A boat tour through the Gemenc Forest is a romantic experience.

▼ In Kalocsa und seiner Umgebung bestimmt der rote Paprika das Leben der Ungarn.
▼ In and around Kalocsa, red peppers play a dominant role in the life of Hungarians.

Die kroatisch-serbische Donau

Auf 137 Flusskilometern streift die Donau das rechtsseitige Kroatien, wo sie wie im linksseitigen Serbien Dunav genannt wird. Es ist eine zauberhafte Landschaft aus Teichen, Kanälen und Galeriewäldern, durchsetzt von Feldern und kleinen Dörfern, die sich mit dem 17.000 Hektar großen Biosphärenreservat Kopacki rit am kroatischen Ufer erstreckt. Seeadler brüten noch in den Sumpfgebieten, ebenso wie Schwarzstörche, und der Bestand an Rotwild ist außerordentlich. Sogar Wildkatzen und Wildschweine kann man noch beobachten, und die UNESCO denkt darüber nach, den Naturpark zum Weltnaturerbe zu ernennen.

Aber die Gegend an der kroatischen Donau ist auch eine zerstörte Landschaft, deren Dörfer und Städte im Krieg zwischen Kroatien und Serbien fast völlig vernichtet wurden. Die

The Croatian-Serbian Danube

The Danube now roams for 137 km (85 miles) with Croatia on its right bank, Serbia on the left, and the river is called the Dunav in both countries. The enchanting landscape consists of ponds, canals and riparian forests interspersed with fields and little villages that stretch across the 17,000 hectare (42,000 acre) of the Kopacki rit Nature Park on the Croatian side of the river. Sea eagles and black storks still nest in the protected swampy areas, and the concentration of red deer is extraordinary. You can even see wildcats and wild boars. UNESCO is considering designating Kopacki Rit as a World Heritage Site.

But the area on the Croatian Danube is also a landscape of ruins, where villages and cities were almost completely destroyed in the war between Croatia and Serbia. The cities of

▾ Auch Kroatien ehrt die Donau mit einer Tafel in Donaueschingen.
▾ Croatia also honors the Danube with a plaque at the spring in Donaueschingen.

▾ Das Biosphärenreservat Kopacki rit am kroatischen Donauufer ist 17.000 Hektar groß.
▾ Kopacki Rit Nature Park on the Croatian side of the Danube encompasses 17,000 hectares (42,000 acres).

▲ Das einst prächtige Schloss von Vukovar liegt nach dem serbischen Beschuss in Trümmern – so wie ein Großteil der Stadt.
▲ After bombardment by the Serbs, the once splendid Castle of Vukovar lies in ruins, as did most of the city.

Städte Vukovar und Osijek gehören dazu, ebenso wie die vielen kleinen Dörfer; sie standen zu Beginn der 1990er-Jahre lange unter serbischem Beschuss, und die Wunden des Krieges sind noch nicht einmal in Ansätzen verheilt. Es ist seit Jahrhunderten eine leid- und kriegsgeprüfte Region: Von Türken wie von Ungarn bereits im 17. Jahrhundert umkämpft, war die Region auch Schauplatz des Ersten Weltkriegs. Wenige Jahre später sah sie im Zweiten Weltkrieg die Kämpfe zwischen Deutschen und Sowjets. Mit der Beendigung des Kroatienkrieges im Jahr 1995 und der damit erlangten Unabhängigkeit hoffen die Kroaten, dass nun Ruhe zwischen Donau und Drau einkehrt. Bis die Wunden verheilt sind, dürfte es dagegen noch Jahrzehnte dauern. Ein Denkmal hat der junge Staat der Donau aber schon einmal gesetzt, mit der Tafel am Quelltopf in Donaueschingen und in seiner Nationalhymne: „auch du Donau, verliere deine Kraft nicht, ... , sage der Welt, dass der Kroate sein Volk liebt!" Die Donau wie das Meer gilt den Kroaten als Verbindung, als Tor zu Europa und zur Welt.

Vukovar and Osijek, as well as many little villages, were among those that were under Serbian fire in the 1990s, and the wounds of war have not yet begun to heal. The region has been afflicted with war and suffering for centuries. The Turks and Hungarians fought over it in the seventeenth century, and it was a theater in World War I. Shortly thereafter, it saw fighting between the Germans and Soviets in World War II. With the end of the Croatian War in 1995, the country finally gained its longed-for independence, and Croats hoped that peace would finally return to the area between the Danube and Drava. But it may take decades for the wounds to heal completely. The young state has already erected a monument, by placing a plaque at the Donau's source in Donaueschingen and in the words of its national anthem: "Oh Danube, do not lose your power, ... and tell the world that a Croat loves his people!" Croatians see the Danube and the sea as conduits, gateways to Europe and to the world.

Kurz hinter der kroatischen Stadt Ilok tritt die Donau endgültig nach Serbien ein. Entsprach das linke, serbische Donauufer bis Ilok landschaftlich in etwa dem rechten, kroatischen – wobei es etwas urbaner war und auch stärker von den Serben als Ausflugsziel genutzt wurde –, so wird die Donaulandschaft hinter der Grenze wieder hügeliger. Es ist die autonome Provinz Vojvodina mit ihrer Hauptstadt Novi Sad, die die Donau nun durchfließt.

Im Habsburgischen Kaiserreich umfasste die Vojvodina ein wesentlich größeres Gebiet von Rumänien bis Ungarn. Vornehmlich dort – in der während der Türkenherrschaft stark entvölkerten Pannonischen Tiefebene – siedelte bereits Prinz Eugen von Savoyen, später Maria Theresia und ihr Sohn Joseph II. Deutsche an, die sogenannten Donauschwaben. In Ulmer Schachteln zogen in den Schwabenzügen zwischen 1692 und 1786 rund 150.000 Schwaben von Ulm aus, um sich

Shortly after the Croatian city of Ilok, the Danube finally enters Serbia. Prior to reaching Ilok, the Serbian side is somewhat more urban and sees a lot of recreational use. Even so, the landscape on the Serbian left bank of the Danube is similar to that of the Croatian right bank. After crossing the border, however, the terrain becomes hillier again. The river now flows through the autonomous province of Vojvodina and its capital, Novi Sad.

In the days of the Habsburg Empire, Vojvodina was a considerably larger territory that extended from Romania to Hungary. Prince Eugene of Savoy as well as Maria Theresa and her son, Joseph II, settled Germans on the Pannonian Plain–which had been largely depopulated during the preceding period of Ottoman rule–who became known as the Donauschwaben, or Danube Swabians. Between 1692 and 1786, around 150,000 Swabians departed from Ulm by boat

▼ „Donau, ... Bringe etwas Luft, von der man nicht vergeht", hofft die verwitterte serbische Tafel an der Donauquelle und spielt auf die Hitze an der südlichen Donau an.
▼ "Danube, ... bring a little air to lessen the sweltering," a weathered Serbian plaque pleads hopefully at the Danube source, alluding to the heat of the southern Danube region.

▼ Novi Sad, die Hauptstadt der Vojvodina, begeistert mit einer hübschen Altstadt und der Festung Petrovaradin.
▼ Novi Sad, capital of Vojvodina, is delightful with its pretty old town and Petrovaradin Fortress.

auf dem Balkan niederzulassen und es durch die Bewirtschaftung des fruchtbaren Landes zu Wohlstand zu bringen – eine Hoffnung, die sich nur für wenige Jahrhunderte erfüllte. Waren die ersten Jahre an der Donau von Not und Armut geprägt, so machten die Donauschwaben bald aus den Sumpfgebieten ein ertragreiches Ackerland, und auch das Handwerk blühte in den Städten. Spätestens mit dem Zweiten Weltkrieg aber war das passé: Als deutsche und nicht vojvodische Bauern angesehen, mussten sie erst vor der Sowjetarmee fliehen oder wurden später von kommunistischen Regimen eingegliedert, mussten serbische, rumänische, ungarische Namen annehmen, Deutsch durfte nicht mehr gesprochen werden.

Die Landschaft auf dem rechten Donauufer um Novi Sad nennt sich Fruska Gora, ein Nationalpark von außerordentlicher Schönheit. Denn in seinen sanften Hügeln sind nicht nur rund 1500 Pflanzenarten – davon etwa 700 Heilkräuter und etwa 150 endemische Arten – angesiedelt, sie sind auch durch-

to settle in the Balkans and seek their fortunes by farming the fertile land. And they were able to prosper for several centuries. The early years on the Danube were filled with poverty and hardship, but the Donauschwaben soon turned the swampy region into bountiful farmland, and tradesmen thrived in the towns. But by World War II at the latest, all of that was over. Perceived as German rather than Vojvodian farmers, they first had to flee the Russian army and were later integrated into Communist regimes. They were forbidden to speak German and forced to assume Serbian, Romanian or Hungarian names.

The area on the right bank of the Danube around Novi Sad is called Fruska Gora, a national park of extraordinary beauty. Approximately 1,500 types of plants grow on its gentle hillsides, including around 700 medicinal herbs and 150 that are endemic to the area. In addition, the landscape is dotted with Serbian Orthodox monasteries, built in the

▼ Das Schwemmland an der serbischen Donau mutet an nebligen Hochwassertagen beinahe mystisch an.
▼ On foggy, high-water days, the alluvial plain along the Serbian Danube seems almost mystical.

▲ Saftige Nahrung finden Schafherden auf den Feuchtwiesen der serbischen Donau ausreichend.
▲ Flocks of sheep find plenty of succulent food in the marshy areas along the Danube in Serbia.

setzt von serbisch-orthodoxen Klöstern, errichtet in ihrem streng byzantinischen Stil und teilweise mit eindrucksvollen Fresken ausgemalt. 35 Klöster wurden hier zwischen dem 12. und 18. Jahrhundert errichtet, 17 davon sind noch erhalten – darunter das Kloster Krusedol mit seinen Ikonen und Wandmalereien aus dem 16. bis 19. Jahrhundert und die kleine, aber sehr eindrucksvolle Kirche von Kloster Staro Hopovo mit ihrer schönen Marienikone.

Das Donauschwemmland an der Fruska Gora und um Novi Sad ist eine ideale Weidefläche für Schafe und Kühe, denn die Auwälder, Feuchtwiesen und Inseln bieten ausreichend Futter und werden kaum bewirtschaftet. Novi Sad dagegen mit seiner Festung Petrovaradin, die Türken wie Habsburger gleichermaßen umkämpften, ist die zweitgrößte Stadt Serbiens und als Messestadt auch eines seiner wirtschaftlichen Zentren. Hier lebt – wie in der ganzen Vojvodina – ein buntes Gemisch unterschiedlicher Völker und ethnischer Gruppen: Ungarn, Kroaten, Serben (die heute die Mehrheit

austere Byzantine style, some of which are embellished with remarkable frescoes. Between the twelfth and eighteenth centuries, thirty-five monasteries were built here, seventeen of which have been preserved. These include the Krusedol Monastery, whose icons date back to the sixteenth through nineteenth centuries, as well as the Staro Hopovo Monastery with beautiful Marian icons in its very impressive church.

The alluvian plain of the Danube in Fruska Gora and around Novi Sad is ideal pasture for cows and sheep. Its riverside forests, marshes and islands are barely cultivated and offer plenty of food for the animals. Novi Sad itself, on the other hand, is Serbia's second largest city, and, with its exhibition center, is an important economic center. Both Turks and Habsburgs fought over Novi Sad and its Petrovaradin Fortress. As is true throughout Vojvodina, a colorful mix of peoples and ethnic groups lives here: Hungarians, Croats, Slovaks, Germans, Romanians, Rusyns, Romani people and

bilden), Slowaken, Deutsche, Rumänen, Russinen, Sinti und Roma. Ein Kulturengemisch, das sich auch in Belgrad, der Hauptstadt Serbiens und vierten Kapitale an der Donau, wiederfindet.

Am Zusammenfluss von Donau und Save (Sava) gelegen, war Belgrad seit den Türkenkriegen eine viel umkämpfte Stadt. 1521 von den Türken erstmals erobert, rückten die Habsburger immer wieder gegen die Stadt vor; die Machtverhältnisse wechselten im Laufe der Jahrhunderte vielfach. Einer der bekanntesten Eroberer ist Prinz Eugen von Savoyen. Seine Inbesitznahme der Stadt im Jahr 1717 mittels einer Pontonbrücke statt über Land wurde in einem bekannten Volkslied verewigt:

„Prinz Eugen, der edle Ritter,
wollt' dem Kaiser wied'rum kriegen
Stadt und Festung Belgerad.
Er ließ schlagen einen Brukken,
daß man kunnt' hinüberrucken
mit'r Armee wohl vor die Stadt."

◄ Byzantinische Baukunst in Belgrad
◄ Byzantine architecture in Belgrade

Serbs, who today are in the majority. This cultural melting pot is also typical of Belgrade, which is the capital of Serbia and the fourth capital city on the Danube.

Located at the confluence of the Dunav and Sava Rivers, Belgrade has been a hotly contested city since the time of the Ottoman Wars. First conquered by the Ottomans in 1521, the Habsburgs advanced on the city time and again, and the balance of power shifted frequently over the course of centuries. Prince Eugene of Savoy was one of the most famous conquerors. His taking of the city in 1717 via a pontoon bridge, rather than by land, was immortalized in a well-known folk song:

Prince Eugene, the noble knight,
wanted to win for the Kaiser
the city and fortress of Belgrade.
He had a bridge built,
o're which they could cross
with'is army right at the gates.

▲ Der Festungshügel in Belgrad von der Savemündung aus gesehen
▲ The fortress on the hill above Belgrade as seen from the confluence of the Sava and Danube

Es ist die Festung auf dem Kalemegdan, hoch über der Donau gelegen und heute immer noch in ihren gewaltigen Ausmaßen dahingestreckt, von der die Rede ist. Schon die Römer errichteten hier – am Save-Donau-Zusammenfluss, dem Tor nach Osten wie Westen – ein Fort, doch war die Gegend wahrscheinlich schon während der Jungsteinzeit besiedelt.

Kriege um diesen strategisch wichtigen Punkt gab es zahlreiche: Neben den Türken und Habsburgern fielen die Hunnen unter Attila über Belgrad her; in der neueren Geschichte waren es die schweren Bombardements des Ersten und Zweiten Weltkriegs und zuletzt im Jahr 1999 die der NATO im Zuge des Kosovokriegs, die die Stadt immer wieder zerstörten. Wenige Gebäude sind daher älter als 100 Jahre, und die Peripherien der Stadt sind – wie in Bratislava und in Budapest – von den grau-braunen sozialistischen und mittlerweile recht maroden Plattenbauten geprägt.

The fortress referred to is the Kalemegdan, an enormous complex and park that is still perched on a ridge high above the Danube today. The Romans built a fort here at the confluence of the Sava and Danube with gates facing east and west. But the area had probably already been settled since the Neolithic age.

Numerous wars have been fought over this strategically important location. In addition to the Habsburgs and Turks, the Huns attacked Belgrade under Attila's command. More recently, heavy bombardments during the First and Second World Wars and, finally, the 1999 NATO air attacks during the War in Kosovo destroyed the city time and again. This explains why very few buildings are more than a hundred years old, and the city's periphery is characterized by the same gray-brown, Soviet-era prefabricated high-rises, by now rather decrepit, that are found in Bratislava and Budapest.

Vom Fluss aus aber hat sich die Ansicht auf Belgrad gar nicht so sehr verändert: Vom gegenüberliegenden Saveufer aus erscheint der Festungshügel – der heute ein öffentlicher Park ist – noch beinahe so wie auf der Darstellung von 1717, die man auf einem Ulmer Haus im Fischerviertel findet. Rund um die Festung erstreckt sich die Stadt – allerdings wesentlich weiter als damals. 1,5 Millionen Einwohner leben heute in der Stadt, zu Beginn des 19. Jahrhunderts waren es gerade einmal 20.000. Die Zahl der Deutschen ist allerdings seit damals stark gesunken: Knapp 500 wurden bei der letzten Volkszählung im Jahr 2002 gezählt. Die eindeutige Mehrheit der Bewohner stellen auch in Belgrad die Serben.

Für Belgrad ist die Save der wichtigere Fluss: Seine städtischen und stadtnahen Ufer sind ein Freizeitparadies, in dem die Belgrader mit ihren Hausbooten anlegen und wo sie die

The view of Belgrade from the river, however, hasn't changed all that much. From Sava on the opposite bank, the fortress on the hill–which is now a public park–still looks nearly as it did in a 1717 painting that adorns an old house in the fishermen's quarter. The city spreads out all around Kalemegdan Fortress, albeit over a much wider area than in the old days. At the beginning of the nineteenth century, there were not more than 20,000 people living in Belgrade; today it boasts 1.5 million inhabitants. But the number of people of German descent has markedly decreased since then: just 500 were counted in the most recent census from 2002. Serbs now constitute a clear majority of Belgrade's residents.

As far as Belgrade is concerned, the Sava is the more important river. Both in the city and just outside of town, its shores are a recreational paradise where people dock their houseboats

▼ Von Ulm zogen die sogenannten Donauschwaben bis hinunter nach Belgrad, und so begann ein reger kultureller Austausch, auf den auch die Ulmer stolz waren. An einem Ulmer Haus in der Altstadt findet sich noch heute eine Darstellung Belgrads von 1717, die Festung, Stadt und den Zusammenfluss von Donau und Save zeigt.

▼ The Danube Swabians traveled from Ulm all the way down to Belgrade. Thus began a lively cultural exchange that the Germans also took pride in. One of their houses in the old part of the city still bears a picture of Belgrade in 1717 that shows the fortress, the city and the confluence of the Danube and Sava Rivers.

▲ Fischern sichert die Donau um Belgrad ein gutes Einkommen.
▲ The Danube provides a good income for fishermen around Belgrade.

Wochenenden verbringen. Die Donau ist ihnen zu wild und ungezähmt, zu gefährlich ist es, in ihr zu baden. Das Fischen dagegen ist an der Donau wesentlich verbreiteter, vor allem hinter dem Zusammenfluss der beiden Flüsse, die nun zu einem einzigen gigantischen Strom angewachsen sind. An manchen Stellen ist die Donau nun bis zu 3 Kilometer breit.

Wie in Belgard selbst so zeugen auch weiter donauabwärts kolossale Festungsruinen von der kriegerischen Geschichte Serbiens: Die Festung von Smederevo war einst Residenz der serbischen Könige und konnte der Belagerung und Beschießung durch die Türken am längsten standhalten. Zur Ruine wurde die Burg erst im Zweiten Weltkrieg. Kurz hinter Smederevo mündet die in Serbien viel besungene Morava in die Donau. Die Donau hat mit Belgrad – der Pforte zum Balkan – nun die Pannonische Tiefebene verlassen, um bald auf Süd-

and spend the weekends. The Danube strikes them as too wild and untamed, and too dangerous to swim in. Fishing, on the other hand, is far more prevalent on the Danube, especially beyond the confluence where the two rivers flow together to become a single, powerful stream. In some places, the Danube is now as much as 3 km (1.9 miles) across.

As in Belgrade, colossal fortress ruins farther downstream on the Danube attest to Serbia's history of armed conflict. Smederevo Fortress, actually a fortified town, was once the residence of the Serbian kings, and was able to withstand the Ottoman siege and attacks longer than any other. The castle didn't actually become a ruin until World War II. Shortly beyond Smederevo, the Morava, much extolled in Serbia, flows into the Danube. In Belgrade, the gateway to the Balkans, the Danube has left the Pannonian Plain and will soon meet the

karpaten und Balkangebirge zu treffen, die sie mit ihren mächtigen Wassern überwinden muss.

Zuvor trifft sie auf eine weitere malerische Festungsruine, Ram bzw. Ramski Grad auf Serbisch. Zwischen den Festungsmauern sind noch zwei letzte Türme auszumachen, der Rest wurde im 18. Jahrhundert zerstört. Die Festungsruine liegt in einer weiten Donauschleife am rechten Flussufer, und ihr gegenüber – bei dem Flusskilometer 1075 – beginnt nun Rumänien. Noch auf 230 Flusskilometern wird die Donau die Grenze zwischen Serbien und Rumänien bilden, und während sie für diese Strecke am rechten Ufer ihren Namen Dunav behält, wird sie am linken, rumänischen Ufer nun zur Dunarea. Und sie wird ab hier die Region der mittleren Donau verlassen und in ihren Unterlauf eintreten – dem Kilometer 0 stetig entgegen.

Southern Carpathians and the Balkan Mountains, both of which must be conquered by her powerful waters.

Prior to that, the Danube encounters one more picturesque ruin – that of Ram Castle. You can still make out the remains of two towers between the fortress walls; the others were destroyed in the eighteenth century. The castle ruins lie on the right bank in a wide bend in the Danube and, across from Ram at kilometer 1075 (mile 668), she arrives in Romania. The Danube River constitutes the border between Serbia and Romania for another 230 km (143 miles). While she is still called the Dunav on the right bank, she will be called the Dunarea on the left bank in Romania. The river is now leaving the middle section of the Danube and entering her lower course, steadily making her way toward kilometer zero.

▾ Gegenüber der serbischen Festungsruine Ram beginnt am linken Donauufer Rumänien.
▾ Across from the ruins of Ram Castle in Serbia, Romania begins on the left bank of the Danube.

Das Eiserne Tor zwischen Serbien und Rumänien

Wer noch vor wenigen Jahrzehnten per Schiff die Donau stromabwärts fuhr, musste zu Recht um sein Leben fürchten: Denn dort, wo sich bei dem rumänischen Moldava Noua heute die Donau zu einem See staut und die mächtige Feste Golubac am serbischen Ufer auftaucht, beginnt das Eiserne Tor, der beeindruckendste und früher gefährlichste Abschnitt an der gesamten Donau.

Zwischen hohen, schroffen Felswänden, die sich teilweise bis zu einer Höhe von 1200 Metern auftürmen, schiebt sich der Strom zwischen den Ausläufern der südlichen Karpaten und dem Balkangebirge hindurch. In seinen Tiefen lauerten dabei Felsriffe und Bergspitzen, und wer bis in die 1970er-Jahre als Schiffer keinen erfahrenen Lotsen an seiner Seite hatte, musste unweigerlich mit der Havarie seines Schiffes rechnen. Nicht wenige Donauschiffer haben hier ihr Leben gelassen.

- Bei der Festung Golubac beginnt das Eiserne Tor.
- The Iron Gate begins near Golubac Fortress.

The Iron Gate Between Serbia and Romania

Just a few years ago, people traveling downriver on the Danube by ship quite rightly feared for their lives. For here, where the flow of the Danube is stemmed to create a lake near the Romanian town of Moldava Noua and the mighty Golubac Fortress appears on the Serbian bank, begins the Iron Gate. This fearsome and impressive series of gorges used to be the most dangerous portion of the entire Danube.

Between rugged, high rock walls that tower 1,200 meters (3,900 feet) high in some places, the river pushes its way through the foothills of the Southern Carpathians and the Balkan Mountains. Rocky reefs and jagged peaks lurked in the depths of the river, and any captain who didn't have an experienced pilot at his side would inevitably have to reckon with damage to his ship. Many a Danube shipman lost his life here.

▲ Im Museumsdorf von Lepenski Vir
▲ In the museum village of Lepenski Vir
▸ Bei Lepenski Vir fanden Archäologen die Siedlung einer unbekannten steinzeitlichen Kultur.
▸ Archaeologists have found remains of the settlement of an unknown Stone Age culture near Lepenski Vir.

Bereits die Römer, die bis hierher ihr Imperium ausgedehnt hatten, versuchten daher, das Tor durch den Bau von Kanälen fahrsicherer zu machen – mit wenig Erfolg. Ein wenig nutzbringender waren da die Sprengungen zahlreicher Untiefen im 19. Jahrhundert. Doch erst der Beginn des Baus eines Kraftwerks donauabwärts machte die Donauschifffahrt im Abschnitt des Eisernen Tors zu einem ungefährlichen Unterfangen, das heute auch ohne Lotsen auskommt.

Im Jahr 1972 begann der Bau des Kraftwerks Djedap I, ein Gemeinschaftsprojekt Rumäniens und des damaligen Jugoslawiens, das kurz vor Drobeta Turnu Severin den Donaudurchbruch abriegelt und das Wasser aufstaut, sodass es an manchen Stellen 90 Meter tief ist. Das macht sich auch 150 Kilometer weiter stromaufwärts – nämlich am Eingang des Tores bei Golubac – bemerkbar. Heute liegt die Donau so friedlich in dem Durchbruch von Karpaten und Balkan, dass

Even the Romans, who had expanded their empire as far as the Iron Gate, had tried to make the gorges safer by building canals, but to no avail. Numerous shelves were blown up in the nineteenth century, which was somewhat more beneficial. But it wasn't until construction began on a power plant downriver that navigation through the Iron Gate on the Danube became a safe undertaking. Today it can even be accomplished without a pilot.

The hydroelectric power plant Djedap I (also known as Iron Gate I), a joint project between Romania and the former Yugoslavia, has been in operation since 1972. The Danube Gorge was blocked shortly before Drobeta Turnu Severin, and the water backed up to a depth of 90 meters (295 feet) in some places. This is noticeable even 150 km (93 miles) upstream at the entrance to the Iron Gate near Golubac. Today, the Danube is so peaceful in the Carpathian-Balkan Gorge

DECEBALUS REX
DRAGAN FECIT

man an einen stillen See erinnert wird. Untiefen und Stromschnellen sind passé, die Schiffe können ungehindert passieren. Donaudampfer mit Touristen machen sich das zunutze, und in den Tiefen stehen die Welse, die ruhige, tiefe Gewässer lieben und hier nur die Donaufischer zum Feind haben.

Sobald man die Feste Golubac passiert hat, kommt man aus dem Staunen nicht mehr heraus: Allein die Landschaft ist atemberaubend. Zwischen den steil abfallenden, in den Himmel aufragenden bewaldeten Bergen und auf dem breiten, stillen Fluss kommt man sich selbst auf einem luxuriösen Kreuzfahrtschiff recht klein vor. Dass sich hier aber auch noch jahrtausendealte Kultur finden lässt, ist völlig unerwartet. Bei Lepenski Vir haben Archäologen vor einigen Jahren eine mittel- bis jungsteinzeitliche Siedlung einer bis dato unbekannten Kultur ausgegraben. Sie lag an der Donau mit Blick auf einen trapezförmigen Felsen im heutigen Rumänien, und so war

that it resembles a still lake. Shoals and rapids are no more, and ships can pass unhindered. Danube steamships for tourists take advantage of this. Catfish love the calm, deep waters, and their only enemies are anglers on the Danube.

As soon as you pass Golubac Fortress, the mind boggles at the sheer beauty of the landscape. As you travel the wide, still river between the wooded hills that drop off steeply and rise high into the sky, even on a luxurious cruise ship you may feel rather small and insignificant. What is entirely unexpected, however, are the remnants of culture stretching back thousands of years. Near Lepenski Vir, archaeologists have unearthed a Middle Stone Age to Neolithic Period settlement of a culture previously unknown. It was located on the Danube in modern-day Romania, within view of a trapezoidal rock, and the layout of the houses was also trapezoidal. But the most astounding discovery of all were the stone

◀ Thrakerkönig Decebal wacht in Stein gehauen über sein einstiges Reich.
◀ The Dacian king Decebal, carved in stone, watches over his former kingdom.
▼ Das hübsche Kloster Mraconia musste dem Stauwasser am Eisernen Tor weichen und wurde ein paar Meter höher wieder aufgebaut.
▼ The lovely Mraconia Monastery had to be moved out of the way of the Iron Gate reservoir and was reassembled at a higher elevation.

▲ So verloren würden selbst größere Schiffe als eine Motoryacht im Eisernen Tor wirken.
▲ Even big ships such as a motorized yacht seem lost in the Iron Gate.

auch der Grundriss der Häuser trapezförmig. Der erstaunlichste Fund aber waren steinerne Statuetten mit wulstigen Fischmäulern. Man kann sie in Belgrad besichtigen, die Ausgrabungen sind noch am Ufer zu sehen.

Nur wenige Kilometer stromabwärts steht auf einem Felsvorsprung auf rumänischer Seite am Kasanpass das schneeweiße Kloster Mraconia, das einmal wesentlich tiefer in der Schlucht lag und dem Stausee weichen musste. Nicht sehr alt, sondern aus dem Jahr 2004, aber dennoch beeindruckend ist der übermächtige, in den Fels gemeißelte Kopf des Königs Decebal. Der letzte König des Thrakerreichs, damals bereits Provinz des Imperium Romanum und Wiege Rumäniens, beging im Jahr 106 Selbstmord, weil er sich dem römischen Kaiser Trajan nicht ergeben wollte. Fährt man an dem Monument vorbei, fühlt man sich ein bisschen an Tolkiens „Der Herr der

statuettes with bulging fish mouths. The statuettes are on display in a museum in Belgrade, and the excavations can still be seen by the river bank.

Just a short way downstream,, the snow-white Mraconia (Mracuna) Monastery sits on a rocky ledge on the Romanian side of the river near the Kazan Pass. The cloister used to stand significantly further down the gorge, but had to make way for the reservoir. Not so old, but nevertheless impressive, is the overpowering head of King Decebalus, which was completed in 2004. The last ruler of the Dacian kingdom, which was already inexorably becoming a province of the Roman Empire and the cradle of Romania, Decebalus committed suicide in 106 CE rather than suffer the humiliation of submitting to Emperor Trajan. Sailing past the monument, you might be reminded of the moment in *The Lord of the Rings*

Ringe" erinnert, wenn die „Gefährten" die Steinstatuen auf dem Anduin passieren. An Trajan erinnert die „Tabula Traiana", die wieder auf serbischer Seite steht und nur vom Wasser aus sichtbar ist. Der Kaiser ließ die Marmortafel im Jahr 100 anlässlich der Fertigstellung einer Straße und Brücke errichten. Auch sie lag tief in der Schlucht und musste vor dem Bau des Kraftwerks versetzt werden, um nicht im Wasser zu versinken. Anderem ist es nicht so gut ergangen, die römische Stadt Orsova etwa ist in den Tiefen der Donau versunken.

Rund um den Fluss mit seinen kulturellen Schätzen breitet sich rechts der Donau auf serbischer Seite der Djerdap-Nationalpark und am linken, rumänischen Ufer der Naturpark Eisernes Tor aus. Auch hier ist die Natur spektakulär, für Abenteurer wie geschaffen. Steile Wege führen durch den

when the "companions" pass the stone statues on the Anduin, Tolkein's Great River of Wilderland.

The Tabula Traiana, a marble tablet on the Serbian side of the river that is only visible from the water, recalls Trajan. The emperor had it built in the year 100 to commemorate the completion of a road and bridge at the Iron Gate. The tablet lay deep in the gorge, and it also had to be moved before the power station was built so that it wouldn't end up underwater. But not everything could be relocated: the Roman city of Orsova, for example, sank below the depths of the Danube.

Surrounding the river with its many cultural treasures are the Djerdap National Park along the right bank of the river in

Mit der „Tabula Traiana" setzte der römische Kaiser Trajan seinem Straßenbau ein bleibendes Denkmal.
The Roman emperor Trajan placed a lasting monument to his road-building project with the Tabula Traiana.

Wald aus Eichen und Hainbuchen, Höhlen liegen dazwischen versteckt, in denen man Tropfsteine bewundern kann und in denen einst Drachen und Ungeheuer gehaust haben sollen. Die gibt es zwar nicht mehr, doch leben – wie man es zumindest auch von den Karpaten nicht anders erwartet – Wölfe, Braunbären und Luchse in den Wäldern. Dazwischen trifft man aber auch auf Anzeichen von Zivilisation: Kleine Dörfer, hübsche Gehöfte, Felder und Weiden laden zum Ausruhen ein.

Auf dem Fluss aber erreichen die Schiffe nun das Kraftwerk Djerdap I. Bei einer Leistung von 3060 Megawatt versorgt es Serbien und Rumänien mit Strom. Die Schiffe müssen sich an einer der beiden Schleusen anstellen, werden in dem 310 Meter langen und 34 Meter breiten Kanal um 16 Meter abgesenkt und treten dann in die Region der unteren Donau ein.

Serbia, and the Iron Gate Nature Preserve on the left bank in Romania. The natural setting is spectacular and tailor-made for adventurers. Steep paths lead through forests of oak and hornbeam, and there are caves hidden among the trees; there you can admire the stalagmites where dragons and monsters supposedly once dwelled. They aren't here anymore, but as one might expect in the Carpathians, wolves, brown bears and lynx do inhabit the forests. You also run into signs of civilization here and there: little villages, lovely farmsteads, fields and meadows invite you to stop and rest.

Back on the river, ships now arrive at the Djerdap I power station, which generates 3,060 megawatts of electric power for Serbia and Romania. Ships have to line up to enter one of the two locks, measuring 310 by 34 meters (52.5 by 111.5 feet), and are lowered 16 meters (52 feet) to enter the Lower Danube.

▾ Einst heimtückischste Stelle für Donauschiffer, gleicht das Eiserne Tor heute an manchen Stellen eher einem ruhigen See.
▾ Once a treacherous place for Danube captains, some stretches of the Iron Gate look more like a peaceful lake today.

Fast unmittelbar nach dem Verlassen von Djerdap I verändert die Donaulandschaft merklich ihr Gesicht: Die hohen Berge ziehen sich zunächst in den Hintergrund zurück, um bald in sanfte Hügel und schließlich sogar in eine weite Ebene überzugehen. Bei der rumänischen Stadt Drobeta Turnu Severin mit ihrem Museum zum Eisernen Tor lässt sich noch einmal alles zur Geschichte und Landschaft des eben durchfahrenen Durchbruchtals erfahren.

Eine zweite Schleuse, Djerdap II, folgt hinter Drobeta Turnu Severin, dann kann die Donau wieder ungehindert ihren Weg nehmen. Bei Flusskilometer 846 trifft die Donau auf das Dreiländereck Serbien, Rumänien und Bulgarien, wo sie nun auch Serbien verlässt. Ihren Namen darf sie dagegen am rechten Flussufer behalten, denn auch die Bulgaren sprechen von der Dunav.

Almost immediately after leaving Djerdap I, the Danube landscape changes markedly. The high mountains retreat into the background for the time being, quickly giving way to gentle hills and finally a wide plain. In the Romanian city of Drobeta Turnu Severin, there is a museum devoted to the Iron Gate, where you can learn all about the history and landscape of the gorge you just passed through.

After passing through Drobeta Turnu Severin there is another lock at Djerdap II, and then the Danube can flow on its merry way again. At kilometer 846 (mile 526) the Danube comes to a triangle where Serbia, Romania and Bulgaria meet. This is also where the river departs Serbia, but she can keep her name on the right bank, because it is also called the Dunav in Bulgaria.

▼ Auch die antike Geschichte des Eisernen Tors wird im Museum von Drobeta Turnu Severin gewürdigt.
▼ The museum in Drobeta Turnu Severin pays tribute to the ancient history of the Iron Gate as well.

Exkurs: Unberechenbare Fluten - Hochwasser an der Donau

Wenn man bedenkt, dass über die Donau ein Großteil des südlichen Mittel- und Südosteuropas entwässert wird, der Fluss aber vielerorts in ein zu enges, künstliches Bett gezwängt wurde, verwundert es nicht, dass sich die Hochwasser an der Donau für die dort lebenden Menschen katastrophal auswirken. Das gilt für die Bewohner an oberer und mittlerer Donau, insbesondere aber für die Balkanländer: Beginnt die Schneeschmelze in den Alpen, Karpaten, auf dem Balkangebirge und in den zahllosen Mittelgebirgen Europas, räumen die Bewohner entlang serbischer, rumänischer und bulgarischer Donau regelmäßig ihre Häuser, ziehen in Notunterkünfte, stapeln Sandsäcke auf durchweichte Deiche und flüchten vor durchbrechenden Deichen. Dies gilt etwa für die Jahre 1999, 2002, 2006 und 2009. Soldaten rücken aus, um die Menschen zu evakuieren, der Notstand wird in vielen Ländern ausgerufen. Der Wassermassen – wie denen im April 2006, als

Excursion: Unpredictable Tides - Flooding on the Danube

When you consider that much of south central and southern Europe drains into the Danube, and that the river is squeezed into a man-made bed that in many places is too narrow, then it's hardly surprising that high water levels on the Danube have catastrophic consequences for the people who live along it. This is true for the inhabitants of the Upper and Middle Danube, but particularly for those in the Balkan countries. When the snow begins to melt in the Alps, the Carpathians, the Balkan Mountains and countless lower European mountain ranges, those who live along the Serbian, Romanian and Bulgarian Danube regularly have to vacate their houses. They move into emergency shelters, stack bags of sand on softened dikes, and flee from levees that give way, as happened in 1999, 2002, 2006 and 2009. Soldiers mobilize to help evacuate people, and a state of emergency is declared in many countries. But no one can master deluges like that of April

▾ Alle Gegenden an der Donau kennen die verheerenden Donauhochwasser, ...
▾ The terrible flooding is familiar all along the Danube, ...

▾ ... wie Linz im Jahr 2002 ...
▾ ... for example in Linz in 2002 ...

am rumänischen Lom statt 8000 Kubikmeter Wasserdurchfluss in der Sekunde 15.200 gemessen wurden – wird dennoch niemand Herr. Die Gründe für die verheerenden Hochwässer sind bekannt: Am gesamten Flussverlauf wurden Stauräume, in denen sich Hochwasser ohne Gefahren ausbreiten kann, deutlich vermindert. Dadurch beschleunigen und erhöhen sich Hochwasserwellen: Durch den Bau von Deichen, Dämmen und Staustufen können sich die Fluten noch weniger ausbreiten. Die Erhöhung der Dämme verbessert zwar den Hochwasserschutz der Anlieger, verschärft aber die Lage derer, die weiter stromabwärts leben und es mit immer größeren und schnelleren Fluten zu tun bekommen. Hinzu kommen die – durch das Waldsterben beschleunigten – Abflüsse des Wassers aus bewaldeten Gegenden sowie der Klimawandel und damit verbunden höhere Verdunstungen und Niederschlagsmengen. Umweltschützer fordern deshalb seit Jahren, dass – statt höherer Dämme – wieder größere Auenlandschaften vor allem an oberer und mittlerer Donau geschaffen werden, in denen sich der Fluss bei Hochwasser ausbreiten kann und was allen Donauanrainern zunutze käme.

2006, when the water flow on the Danube at Lom, Bulgaria, was measured at 15,200 cubic meters (over 4 million gallons) per second, rather than the typical 8,000 cubic meters (2 million gallons). The reasons for the devastating floods are well known. Retention basins have been significantly reduced along the entire course of the river, resulting in higher, faster flood waves. Construction of levees, dams and barrages further limit places where the waves can spread out. And while raising dams improves flood protection for those nearby, it also worsens the situation for those living further downstream, who have to deal with bigger, faster floods. Additional causes include runoff from wooded areas, accelerated by the death of the forests as well as the higher rates of evaporation and precipitation that are associated with climate change. For years, environmentalists have therefore urged the reestablishment of larger riverside meadowlands in lieu of higher dams, particularly on the Upper and Middle Danube. Meadows would allow the river to spread out during periods of flooding and would benefit all who live adjacent to the Danube.

▾ ... oder Budapest im Jahr 2006.
▾ ... and Budapest in 2006.

▾ Nirgends aber trifft es die Menschen schlimmer und häufiger als an der unteren Donau.
▾ But nowhere do people feel the impact more strongly or more often than on the Lower Danube.

▲ Mit 1075 Flusskilometern hat Rumänien den größten Anteil an der Donau.
▲ With 1,075 km (668 miles), Romania can claim the largest share of the Danube.

Die rumänisch-bulgarische Donau

Die Donau wird nun – bis zu ihrer Mündung ins Schwarze Meer – Rumänien nicht mehr verlassen. Mal gehört dem Staat nur das linke, mal nur das rechte Ufer, an anderen Stellen durchfließt die Donau das Land, doch mit insgesamt 1075 Flusskilometern hat Rumänien eindeutig von allen Anrainern den größten Anteil an dem Strom. Landschaftliche Höhepunkte sind der Donaudurchbruch am Eisernen Tor und das riesige Delta.

Mit der Walachei, die sich nun am linken, weiterhin rumänischen Ufer auftut, tritt die Donau dagegen nicht unbedingt in ihre spannendsten Landstriche ein. Eigentlich eine Steppenlandschaft, wird die Walachei seit Beginn des 20. Jahrhunderts intensiv bewässert und seitdem stark landwirtschaftlich genutzt.

The Romanian-Bulgarian Danube

From here on, the Danube will remain in Romania until it flows into the Black Sea. In some places only the left or right bank of the river belongs to Romania; in other places, Romania embraces the Danube from both sides. Of all the countries on the Danube, however, Romania clearly has the largest share of it, with a total of 1075 km (668 miles). The Danube Gorge at the Iron Gate and the huge delta are some of the scenic highlights.

As the Walachia region opens up on the Romanian left bank, however, the Danube enters stretches of land that are admittedly less than thrilling. Walachia is actually a steppe that has been intensively irrigated since the beginning of the twentieth century and cultivated extensively ever since.

Die Uferregionen aber werden von Sumpfwiesen und Auwäldern gesäumt; ab und an musste die Natur den Eingriffen des Menschen weichen, wenn dieser den Fluss stark begrenzt hat und damit eine eher öde Landschaft zurückgelassen hat. Die Fließgeschwindigkeit hat nun deutlich abgenommen, und die Donau strömt in majestätischer Ruhe vor sich hin.

Anders als die Hauptstädte der vorangegangenen Länder ist die rumänische Kapitale keine Donaustadt. Bukarest liegt knapp 70 Kilometer von der Donau entfernt, zwischen den Ausläufern der Karpaten und der Walachei. Dennoch wird es zumindest bei keiner Donaukreuzfahrt, die bis zum Schwarzen Meer führt, ausgelassen. Zu Recht, denn die Metropole ist – wenn auch nicht in jeder Hinsicht schön – so doch äußerst interessant. 1977 wurde Bukarest von einem schweren Erdbeben erschüttert und ein Teil der schönen historischen Stadt mit ihren prächtigen Palais der Belle Epoque zerstört.

But the shores are lined with swampy meadows and alluvial forests. Every now and then, nature has been forced to give way to human intervention, even if this has severely restricted the river and left a rather bleak landscape in its wake. The flow rate has decreased significantly, and the Danube flows along with majestic repose.

Unlike the countries the river's course has previously traversed, the capital of Romania is not situated on the Danube. Bucharest lies 70 km (43.5 miles) away from the Danube, between the foothills of the Carpathians and Walachia. Yet no Danube cruise to the Black Sea would ever leave it off the itinerary, and for good reason. Although it's not beautiful in every respect, Bucharest is still extremely interesting. A powerful earthquake rocked Bucharest in 1977, and part of the beautiful historic city with its magnificent palaces of the Belle Epoque was destroyed.

▼ Eine Fischerhütte an der rumänischen Donau
▼ A fisherman's hut on the Romanian Danube

Das nutzte der Diktator Nicolae Ceausescu, einige seiner monumentalen Bauvorhaben durchzusetzen: etwa den absurd-riesigen Palast des Volkes, für dessen knapp 400.000 Quadratmeter Gesamtfläche etwa ein Fünftel der Stadt abgerissen wurde. 30.000 Menschen arbeiteten täglich an dem Bau, der angeblich immer noch nicht ganz fertig ist. Heute tagt in dem Bau das Parlament, aber auch Ausstellungsräume sind in den etwa 300 stuck- und marmorverzierten Sälen zu finden. Den dafür zum Opfer gefallenen Stadtteil nennen die Bukarester heute „Hiroshima". Wer dieses aber verlässt, der kann noch immer das „Paris des Ostens" erleben mit seinem Fürstenhof, der Stavropoleos-Kirche, dem alten Handelsviertel oder dem reizenden Dorfmuseum am Herastrau-See.

Unweit von Bukarest liegt übrigens das Kloster Snagov: Dort soll sich das Grab von Vlad III. Draculea befinden, der von 1456 bis 1462 und noch einmal im Jahr 1476 Wojwode, also Heerführer, des Fürstentums Walachei war. Der für seine grausamen Pfählungen berühmte Vlad soll Vorbild für Bram Stokers Romanfigur Dracula gewesen sein.

◄ Der Größenwahn des rumänischen Diktators Nicolae Ceausescu lässt sich heute noch gut an seinem monumentalen Palast des Volkes ablesen.
◄ The megalomania of Romanian dictator Nicolae Ceausescu is still prominently on display in his monumental People's Palace.

Romanian dictator Nicolae Ceausescu took advantage of that to push through some of his monumental building plans. Approximately one-fifth of the city was demolished, for example, to build the absurdly gigantic, nearly 400,000 square meter (over 4 million square foot, or almost 100 acre) People's Palace. Thirty thousand people worked on the building every day, and they say it is still not completely finished. It now houses the Parliament, but there is also ample space for exhibition within its 300 or so stucco and marbled halls. The people of Bucharest call the part of town that was sacrificed "Hiroshima." But once you leave this behind, you can still experience the "Paris of the East" with its Old Princely Court, Stavropoleos Church, the old commercial district and the charming outdoor museum (Village Museum) on Lake Herastrau.

Not far from Bucharest is the Snagov Monastery, where the grave of Vlad III Dracula is supposedly located. He was the voivode (ruler) of the Principality of Walachia from 1456 to 1462, and again in 1476. Famous for his cruel impalements, Vlad may have served as inspiration for the main character in Bram Stoker's novel, *Dracula*.

Erstreckt sich auf rumänischer Seite die weite Ebene der Walachei, so sind es auf bulgarischer Seite die sachten Ausläufer von Westbalkan und Hohem Balkan, die die Landschaft um die Donau bestimmen. Weinberge, Obstgärten und Felder ziehen sich durch die Hügel, kleine Dörfer liegen dazwischen. Steilufer grenzen Land und Wasser ab, schmale Auen, Felsenbiotope und die schluchtenartigen Täler in den Nebenflüssen Lom und Jantra beherbergen eine Vielfalt an Tier- und Pflanzenarten. Kilometerweit zieht sich diese Idylle und ist doch – wie die Galeriewälder und Reste von Altauen auf rumänischer Seite – stark bedroht.

Als internationale Wasserautobahn und unter dem Druck der übrigen Anrainerstaaten sind weitere Ausbauten, Kanalisierungen und Begradigungen geplant, die das Befahren der Donau für Schiffe verbessern sollen.

The wide plains of Walachian stretch out on the Romanian side of the river, but the gentle foothills of the western and central Balkan Mountains dominate the Danube landscape. Vineyards, orchards and fields cover the hillsides, with little villages between them. Steep banks separate land from water. Narrow leas, rocky biotopes and gorge-like valleys of the Lom and Jantra tributaries provide habitat for a multitude of plant and animal species. This idyll extends for miles, yet it is critically endangered, as are the riverside forests and what remains of river meadows on the Romanian side.

Under pressure from neighboring countries, plans have been made for further developments, canalizations and straightening of this internationally important waterway that would improve travel on the river for ships.

▾ Die Quelltafel Bulgariens in Donaueschingen
▾ Bulgaria's plaque at the Donaueschingen source

▾ Liebliche Hügel und Steilufer bestimmen die bulgarische Donau.
▾ The Bulgarian Danube is characterized by gentle hills and steep banks.

▲ Das Donauufer in Vidin ist von Beton eingefasst.
▲ The shore of the Danube in Vidin is enclosed in concrete.

Nicht einmal 100 Kilometer hinter Djedap II sind diese Begradigungen deutlich zu sehen. Vidin, das trotz der jahrhundertelangen Zerstörungen durch Römer, in den Türkenkriegen und im Zweiten Weltkrieg auf wundersame Weise architektonisch wie kulturell orientalische mit europäischen Traditionen mischt, ist städtebaulich auch durch den Pragmatismus des Sozialismus bzw. die auch im Westen üblichen Fehler der 1950er- bis 70er-Jahre geprägt.

Die Donau ist in ein starres Bett aus Beton eingefasst, Industrie und Wohnsilos sind außerhalb der Altstadt das bestimmende Moment. Am rumänischen Ufer zeigt die Stadt Calafat ein ebensolches Bild. Die beiden Städte verbindet eine Fähre miteinander, die eine der an der unteren Donau nur noch seltenen Überquerungen möglich macht. Wenn man an die verschwenderische Zahl der Brücken an oberer und mitt-

Not even 100 km (60 miles) beyond Djedap II, this straightening of the river is plain to see. Despite centuries-long destruction by the Romans and in the Ottoman Wars and World War II, Vidin, Bulgaria, is a wondrous mixture of Oriental and European architectural and cultural traditions. From a town planning perspective, it is also marred by socialist pragmatism as well as the errors typical of the 1950s through 1970s in the West.

The Danube is enclosed in a stiff bed of concrete, and beyond the old part of the city, industrial tracts and high-rise ghettos are the dominant features. On the Romanian bank, the city of Calafat presents the same picture. The two cities are connected by a ferry, one of only a few, infrequent possibilities for crossing the Lower Danube. Considering the extravagant number of bridges on the Upper and Middle

▲ Zerfall und Zerstörung schaffen manchmal auch ganz eigene Idyllen, wie hier die Ruine eines einstigen Gotteshauses in Vidin.
▲ Disintegration and destruction can sometimes create idyllic spots, such as the ruins of a former church in Vidin shown here.

lerer Donau denkt (allein in Budapest sind es neun), wundert es, dass an der gesamten unteren Donau nur zwei Brücken über den Fluss führen.

Doch aller Kanalisierung und Eindämmung zum Trotz kann man an der unteren Donau herrliche Naturräume entdecken, zumal zahlreiche Umweltorganisationen für die Renaturierung der Region eintreten und mit ihren Forderungen nicht mehr auf taube Ohren stoßen. Zu sehr zeigen die Hochwasser der letzten Jahre, dass ein weiteres Ausbauen der Donau katastrophale Folgen haben würde. Je weiter man in die Nähe der bulgarischen Stadt Russe – der fünftgrößten Stadt des Landes – kommt, desto natürlichere Gegenden sieht man. Etwa 60 Inseln reihen sich hier aneinander, und durch die Kiese und Sande, die die Donau mit sich führt, werden es immer mehr. Die Insel vor Vardim kann noch völlig intakte Auwälder ihr Eigen nennen, andere Inseln sind auf dem bes-

Danube—there are nine in Budapest alone—it's astonishing that only two bridges still span the Danube in its entire lower section.

Still, despite all the canalization and containment, there are still wonderful natural places to be discovered on the Lower Danube, especially since numerous environmental organizations are speaking out in favor of rehabilitating the region's natural ecosystems. And their demands are no longer falling on deaf ears. The floods of recent years indicate all too clearly that further alterations to the Danube would have catastrophic consequences. The closer you come to Bulgaria's fifth largest city, Ruse, the more natural areas you will see. Around sixty islands are strung together here, and with all the rocks and silt the Danube carries along with it, that number is growing. The island before Vardim can still claim fully intact riparian forests. Other islands, such as Batim, are on the way

ten Weg dorthin, werden aber auch landwirtschaftlich genutzt, wie die Insel Batim. Zuvor aber fährt man mit dem Schiff an der Insel Belene vorbei, die hinter ihren schönen Auwäldern einen Ort des Schreckens verbirgt: 1941 wurde hier ein Konzentrationslager errichtet, das von den Kommunisten 1944 in ein ebenso grausiges Arbeitslager für politische Gefangene umgewandelt wurde. Tausende Inhaftierte verhungerten hier oder starben an Erschöpfung. Heute gibt es hier noch immer ein „normales" Gefängnis.

Mit Russe erreicht man nicht nur die Heimatstadt des Literatur-Nobelpreisträgers Elias Canetti, sondern auch ein Kleinod an der unteren Donau. Seit der Gründerzeit eine wichtige Handelsstadt, brachten die Einwohner Russes ihren Wohlstand zum Ausdruck, indem sie eine Stadt im „europäischen Stil" errichteten: Die Gründerzeitgebäude orientierten sich an den großen Donaustädten Wien und Budapest. Und

to similar states, but are also used for agriculture. Prior to that, however, boats pass Belene Island, whose beautiful riverside forests mask a place of terror. In 1941, a concentration camp was erected here that was converted by the communists in 1944 into an equally grim labor camp for political prisoners. Thousands of the people incarcerated starved to death or died of exhaustion. There is still a "normal" prison on the island today.

Ruse is not only the birthplace of Elias Canetti, winner of the Nobel Prize for Literature, but also a jewel on the Lower Danube. An important commercial center since the Gründerzeit, the residents of Ruse expressed their prosperity by building a "European-style" city. Ruse's nineteenth-century buildings were modeled after the great Danube cities of Vienna and Budapest. Even if Ruse will never be as big as these metropolises, it's still thoroughly enjoyable to stroll through it

▼ Mit Pferd und Wagen wird in Bulgarien noch häufig gewirtschaftet. Neues Gerät kann man sich meist nicht leisten.
▼ People still farm with horse and wagon in Bulgaria. Many people cannot afford more modern equipment.

Exkurs: Knapp 2000 Kilometer in 15 Tagen - die Donaukreuzfahrt

Es ist noch nicht lange möglich, die Donau auf ihrer ganzen Länge bzw. von Passau bis zum Schwarzen Meer entlangzuschippern, trennte doch der Eiserne Vorhang Europa jahrzehntelang. Doch mit dessen Fall kann man die einst klassische Donaukreuzfahrt, die von Passau nach Wien und wieder zurück führte, nun um einiges erweitern: Bis zum Schwarzen Meer tragen uns die Donauwellen und der kräftige Motor unseres Schiffes, der MS Flamenco, in wenigen Tagen; nach nur zwei Wochen ist man schon wieder zurück in Passau. Doch hektisch geht es auf solch einer Reise dennoch nicht zu: Sehr gemächlich ziehen die schönen Kirchen und Klöster, Burgen und Schlösser, die lieblichen Auwälder und mächtigen Donaudurchbruchtäler an unserem Auge vorbei, während wir auf dem Sonnendeck einen Tequila Sunrise trin-

Excursion: 1,240 Miles in Fifteen Days - Cruising the Danube

It wasn't so long ago that it became possible to sail the entire length of the Danube River from Passau to the Black Sea. For decades, the Iron Curtain divided Europe. Now that it has fallen, however, you can extend your Danube cruise beyond the once classic trip from Passau to Vienna and back. The waves of the Danube and the powerful engine of our ship, the MS Flamenco, will carry us all the way to the Black Sea in a few days, and we'll be back in Passau in just two weeks.

Yet such a trip is anything but hectic. As we drink a tequila sunrise on the sun deck, the beautiful churches, monasteries, castles, lovely riverside forests and mighty valleys of the Danube Gorge pass very slowly before our eyes. Sometimes

▼ Eine der beliebtesten Anlegestellen auf einer Donaukreuzfahrt: Esztergom in Ungarn
▼ Ezstergom, Hungary, is one of the most popular stops on a Danube cruise.

ken. Manchmal steigen wir aus, machen eine Besichtigungstour durch Wien, Budapest und Belgrad, genießen die Ruhe und die Tierwelt des Deltas oder essen paprikascharfe Fischsuppe in Kalocsa.

Dem Schengener Abkommen ist es dabei zu verdanken, dass wir nur wenige Zollkontrollen über uns ergehen lassen müssen, dem Bau des Djerdapkraftwerks und den Regulierungen an diesem Donaudurchbruch, dass wir heil das Eiserne Tor passieren können. Dass die Kreuzfahrten die Donau hinab in erster Linie von einem älteren Publikum gebucht werden, liegt beileibe nicht daran, dass die Fahrten langweilig wären. Es gibt kaum eine abwechslungsreichere Art, den europäischen Osten kennenzulernen, und auch auf dem Viersterneschiff wird einiges an Unterhaltung geboten. Der Preis von etwa 3000 Euro (je nach Kabinenstandard) – wenn man Ausflüge und Getränke einrechnet – könnte da wohl abschreckender sein.

we get off the ship for a sightseeing tour of Vienna, Budapest or Belgrade, to enjoy the peacefulness and wildlife of a delta, or to eat spicy paprika fish soup in Kalocsa.

We have the Schengen Agreement to thank for the fact that we have to endure fewer customs checks. The construction of the Djerdap Power Station and the regulation of the Danube Gorge assure safe passage through the Iron Gate. The fact that cruises down the Danube are booked mainly by a mature clientele is certainly not an indication that these trips are boring. There is hardly a more interesting and varied way to get to know eastern Europe, and the four-star ship offers some nice entertainment besides. When you take excursions and drinks into account, and depending on the type of cabin you select, The price tag of approximately 3,000 euros (depending on the type of cabin you book), including excursions and drinks, though substantial, could be worse.

▾ Ob bei einer Kreuzfahrt oder einem kleinen Schiffsausflug: Die Donau ist beinahe immer und überall sehenswert.
▾ Whether on a cruise or day trip on a small boat, the Danube is worth seeing, anytime and anywhere.

auch wenn Russe niemals die Ausmaße solcher Metropolen erreichen konnte, ist es doch hübsch, hindurchzuschlendern und die stuckverzierten Fassaden – die in den letzten Jahren liebevoll restauriert wurden – zu betrachten. Zumal Russe auch am Rande des Naturparks Russenski Lom liegt und damit eine schöne Umgebung bietet.

Zwischen engen Felsschluchten und Auwäldern erstreckt sich der 2930 Hektar große Park, der nicht nur eine intakte Natur mit einer hohen Artenvielfalt aufweist, sondern auch spektakuläre Höhlenklöster und die Felsenkirche von Ivanovo.

Einsiedler zog es ab dem 12. Jahrhundert in die Abgeschiedenheit des Flusstales des Russenski Lom, dessen Felsenhöhlen, die schließlich ganze Klosterkomplexe bildeten, sie bewohnten. Von den rund 250 Kirchen mit ihren Fresken sind einige, wie die des Klosters „Hl. Erzengel Michael", noch gut erhalten, das Kloster „Sveti Dimitar Bassarbovski" sogar noch bewohnt.

and admire the stucco facades that have been so lovingly restored in recent years, all the more so since Ruse the Rusenski Lom Nature Park, just outside the city limits, offers a beautiful setting.

The large park stretches out between narrow gorges and alluvial forests that span 2,930 hectares (7,237 acres). Not only does it boast an intact natural environment with high biodiversity, but is also home to spectacular monastic caves and the rock-hewn churches of Ivanovo. Famed for its medieval frescoes, the complex is a UNESCO World Heritage Site.

The seclusion of the Russenski Lom River Valley has attracted hermits since the twelfth century. They inhabited its rocky caves, which finally became monasteries. Among the 250 churches with frescoes, the Monastery of St. Michael the Archangel is among several whose medieval artwork is well preserved. And the Monastery of Sveti Dimitar Bassarbovski is still lived in to this day.

◄ Russe, das städtische Kleinod an der unteren Donau, liegt nahe dem herrlichen Naturpark Russenski Lom. ▼
◄ The city of Ruse, a jewel on the Lower Danube, is situated near the beautiful Rusenski Lom Nature Park. ▼

Zwischen Silistra und dem Schwarzen Meer

130 Flusskilometer hinter Russe erreicht die Donau die Grenzstadt Silistra, wo sie sich von Bulgarien trennt und nun erst einmal ganz Rumänien gehört. Hier teilt sie sich auch in zwei Arme, verzweigt sich, bildet kleine Kanäle und deutet damit bereits an, was sie bald sein wird: ein riesiges Flussdelta. Außerdem wechselt sie noch einmal den Kurs und fließt statt weiter nach Osten bis kurz vor dem Delta in nördliche Richtung. Die Landschaft am rechten Ufer nennt sich Dobrudscha oder rumänisch Dobrogea, ein teils in Bulgarien, zum größeren Teil aber in Rumänien liegender Landstrich. Sie erstreckt sich östlich der Donau bis zum Schwarzen Meer und bis zum Donaudelta.

In den Sumpfgebieten der Dobrudscha finden Torfstecher und Fischer ihr Auskommen, auch ein wenig Landwirtschaft wird betrieben, denn die Gegend ist relativ fruchtbar. Am westlichen Ufer erstreckt sich der Baragan, eine fruchtbar

Between Silistra and the Black Sea

Travel 130 km (81 miles) beyond Ruse and you will reach the port city of Silistra, where the Danube parts company with Bulgaria and lies entirely in Romania for the time being. The Danube splits into two branches here, spreads out and forms little channels. These are already an indication that she will soon become a vast river delta.

Instead of heading further east, the river also changes course again and flows in a northerly direction until shortly before the delta. The landscape on the right bank is called Dobruja (Dobrogea in Romanian), a region that lies partly in Bulgaria but is mainly on Romanian soil. It stretches eastward along the Danube to the Danube delta and the Black Sea.

Fishermen and peat farmers make their living in the marshes of Dobruja. Since the region is relatively fertile, people also farm the land to a lesser extent. The Baragan Steppe

Mit ihren traditionellen Häusern ▼ und der ebenso althergebrachten Art der Landwirtschaft ▶ ist die Dobrudscha noch sehr urtümlich.
With its traditional houses ▼ and equally old-fashioned farming practices, ▶ Dobruja is still rustic and quaint.

▲ Der Donau-Schwarzmeer-Kanal mag nützlich sein, schön ist er eher selten.
▲ The Danube-Black Sea Canal may be useful, but is seldom attractive.

gemachte Steppenlandschaft. Beide Gebiete – Dobrudscha und Baragan – werden von Bauern besiedelt, die ganz unterschiedlicher Abstammung sind: rumänisch, bulgarisch, tartarisch, türkisch, lippowarisch. Auch Zigeuner, Griechen und die Urenkel der Dobrudschadeutschen leben hier – alle in eher ärmlichen Verhältnissen, aber ihre gemeinsamen, jahrhundertealten Traditionen pflegend.

Unterbrochen wird die ländliche Ruhe und Schönheit durch den Donau-Schwarzmeer-Kanal, der von Cernavoda am rechten Donauarm bis Constanta am Schwarzen Meer führt. Kanal der Tränen oder der Toten wird der Kanal auch genannt, dessen Bau im Jahr 1948 begann und den die Kommunisten dazu nutzten, unliebsame politische Gegner auszuschalten. Denn der Kanalbau war eher ein Zwangsarbeiterlager als eine gewöhnliche Baustelle: Mehrere Zehntausend Häftlinge schufteten zwölf Stunden täglich unter schlimmsten Arbeitsbedingungen. Mit Spitzhacke und Schaufel wurde hier ein 64,2 Kilometer langer Schifffahrtskanal gegraben.

stretches out along the western bank and has been made into agricultural land. Both regions—Baragan and Dobruja—are inhabited by farmers of widely varying origins, including Romanians, Bulgarians, Tartars, Turks and Lippovans. Gypsies, Greeks and the great-grandchildren of Dobrujan Germans live here. Though they all live rather impoverished circumstances, they cultivate their common, centuries-old traditions.

The rural tranquility and beauty of the region are interrupted by the Danube-Black Sea Canal, which runs from the right branch of the Danube at Cernavoda to Constanta on the Black Sea. Construction of the canal began in 1948. Also called the Canal of Tears or Canal of the Dead, the communists used it to get rid of unwelcome political opponents.

In fact, the canal was more of a forced labor camp than an ordinary construction site. Tens of thousands of prisoners toiled twelve hours per day under horrible working conditions. They dug a 64.2 km (39 mile) long shipping canal here

Mehr als 10.000 Menschen starben dabei, an Überanstrengung oder weil sie erschossen wurden. Diktator Ceaucescu ließ zur feierlichen Eröffnung 1984 ein Ehrenmal errichten – aber nicht etwa zu Ehren der Toten, sondern um die Herrlichkeit der Kommunisten und ihr technisches Können zu feiern. Ein Denk- und Ehrenmal für die Opfer des Kanals wurde erst nach Ende des Kommunismus errichtet.

Bei Constanta mündet der Kanal ins Schwarze Meer. Die Stadt ist dadurch einerseits ein mächtiger internationaler Hafen und als solcher von Industrie geprägt. Andererseits aber kann sie auf eine Geschichte zurückblicken, die bereits im 6. Jahrhundert vor Christus begann. Daker, Skythen und Kelten haben diese ebenso mitgeprägt wie Römer, Tartaren, Bulgaren, Griechen, Türken und natürlich Rumänen. Das sieht man noch heute in ihren antiken Ruinen und im Archäologischen Museum (in dem sich übrigens auch zwei Statuen aus dem

with pickaxes and shovels. More than ten thousand men died in the process, either shot or dying of overexertion. Dictator Ceausescu had a memorial built for the opening ceremony in 1984 that did not honor the dead, but instead celebrated the communists and their technical feats. A memorial to honor the victims of the canal was only built after the end of communism.

The canal flows into the Black Sea at Constanta. On the one hand, this makes it a powerful international port, and thus a predominantly industrial city. On the other hand, Constanta can look back on a history that stretches back to the sixth century BCE. Dacians, Scythians and Celts have helped to shape it as much as the Romans, Tartars, Bulgarians, Greeks, Turks and, naturally, the Romanians. This is evident even today in the ancient ruins, mosques and Orthodox churches. Constanta has an archaeological museum in which

▾ Das Casino von Constanta direkt an der Schwarzmeerküste wurde zur Wende zum 20. Jahrhundert errichtet.
▾ The Constanta Casino was built right on the coast of the Black Sea at the turn of the twentieth century.

▲ Am Pruth verläuft die Grenze zwischen Rumänien und Moldawien, das erst seit dem Jahr 2004 einen knappen linksseitigen Flusskilometer besitzt.
▲ Prut is on the boundary between Romania and Moldova, which gained control of less than a kilometer of the river in 2004.

5. Jahrtausend vor Christus, die in Cernavoda gefunden wurden, befinden), an den Moscheen und orthodoxen Kirchen. Ein Großteil der inneren Stadt aber wurde zur Zeit der Wende vom 19. zum 20. Jahrhundert errichtet.

Zurück zur Donau: Sie fließt nun weitverzweigt und kleinere seeartige Buchten bildend weiter Richtung Norden. Wenn sie die Stadt Braila erreichen, verbinden sich die beiden Flussarme noch einmal für einige Kilometer zu einem mächtigen Strom, der 20 Kilometer weiter, bei Flusskilometer 150, Galati erreicht. Bis hierher – vom Schwarzen Meer aus gerechnet – können auch Hochseeschiffe die Donau befahren, sodass man den Fluss hier eigentlich in Seemeilen misst.

Elf Kilometer weiter erreicht man am linken Flussufer Moldawien, dem man indes nur einen kurzen Gruß zuwinken

▲ Nach der Unabhängigkeit ließ auch die Ukraine einen Donaugruß an der Quelle in Donaueschingen anbringen.
▲ Since gaining independence, Ukraine has also mounted a plaque "greeting" the Danube at its source in Donaueschingen.

two statues from the fifth millennium BCE that were discovered in Cernavoda are now housed there. But much of the downtown was erected at the turn of twentieth century.

Returning to the Danube, it now flows in a northerly direction with its branches far apart, forming small, lake-like bays as it goes. When it reaches the city of Braila, the two branches of the river converge into a mighty stream for a ways until 20 km (12.5 miles) farther on the Danube reaches Galati at the 150 kilometer (93 mile) mark. Even ocean-going ships can navigate the Danube up to this point, starting at the Black Sea, so that here the river is actually measured in nautical miles.

You will reach Moldova on the left bank of the river 11 km (6.8 miles) further downstream. You won't have time to do

kann, bevor man es zwölf Kilometer hinter Galati auch schon wieder verlassen hat, um am linken Ufer in die Ukraine einzureisen. Moldawien bzw. die Republik Moldau ist erst seit dem Jahr 1991 unabhängige Republik und besitzt erst seit dem Jahr 2004 genau 0,924 Kilometer Anteil an der Donau. Die Ukraine hatte in einem Gebietsaustausch ein paar Hundert Meter an die junge Republik abgetreten, die seit 1995 in Giurgiulesti einen Donauhafen errichtet.

Wenn die Donau die Ukraine erreicht, dort nun wieder Dunaj heißt und endgültig gen Osten fließt, beginnt das ausgedehnte Donaudelta. Kurz vor Tulcea, einer Hafenstadt im rumänischen Teil des Deltas, teilt sich die Donau in zwei Arme, den Chilia-Arm und den Sulina-Arm. Der Chilia-Arm bildet die Grenze zwischen Rumänien und der Ukraine, der Sulina-Arm ist der für die Großschifffahrt am besten geeignete Arm, weil er – obwohl er am wenigsten Wasser führt – weniger Verlandungen kennt.

more than wave a quick greeting to Moldova before leaving it behind just 12 km (7.5 miles) beyond Galati, at which point Ukraine is on the left bank. The Republic of Moldova has only been an independent republic since 1991, and since 2004 has owned the rights to precisely 0.924 kilometers (0.57 miles) of the Danube. The Ukraine ceded this short stretch to the young republic in a territorial exchange, and Moldova started building a port in Giurgiulesti in 1995.

When the Danube reaches Ukraine, where it is once again called the Dunaj and flows definitively eastward, the expansive Danube delta begins. Shortly before Tulcea, a port city in the Romanian part of the delta, the Danube splits into two branches, the Chilia and the Sulina. The Chilia branch forms the border between Romania and Ukraine. Although it contains a smaller volume of water, the Sulina branch is more suitable for large ships, because it silts up less often.

▼ Der Hafen von Tulcea ist inmitten des Deltas ein wichtiger Warenumschlagplatz.
▼ The port of Tulcea is an important transshipment point in the middle of the Danube delta.

▼ Golden leuchten die Kuppeln der orthodoxen Kirche im Hafen von Izmail.
▼ The gleaming golden domes of the Orthodox church in the harbor of Izmail.

▲ Zu den vielen Tierarten der Donaumündung zählt auch der Biber, der in vielen anderen Regionen Europas vom Aussterben bedroht ist.
▲ Among the myriad animals found on the Lower Danube is the beaver, which is endangered in many other parts of Europe.

Hinter Tulcea zweigt vom Sulina-Arm ein weiterer Hauptarm ab, der Sankt-Georgs-Arm, der bei Sfantu Gheorghe ins Schwarze Meer mündet.

Diese drei Hauptarme bilden zusammen mit dem dichtverzweigten Netz aus Seitenarmen, Altarmen, Seen, schwimmenden Inseln, Röhrichten, Galerie- und Auwäldern das zweitgrößte Flussdelta Europas. Nur etwa 20 Prozent des knapp 5000 Quadratkilometer großen Gebiets bestehen aus Land, der Rest sind Gewässer. Etwa 5000 Tierarten leben in dem Biosphärenreservat, das 1991 von der UNESCO zum Weltnaturerbe ernannt wurde. Allein 325 Vogelarten – darunter Kormoranen, Pelikanen, den Wappenvögeln des Deltas, Silberreihern, Seeschwalben und Seeadlern – dient das Delta als Lebensraum oder zumindest Brut-, Rast- und Nahrungsplatz. Kein Wunder bei etwa 50 Fischarten und der mit 18.000 Hektar größten Schilflandschaft der Welt. Es ist ein Naturparadies, dessen Schutz sich Rumänien, die Ukraine und

After Tulcea, an additional main branch splits off from the Sulina, the St. George, which flows into the Black Sea at Sfantu Gheorghe, Romania.

Europe's second largest river delta is composed of these three main branches together with a dense network of minor branches, oxbow and other lakes, floating islands, reed beds, riparian forests and riverside meadows. Only about 20 percent of the nearly 5,000 square km (1,930 square mile) area consists of land; the rest is water. An estimated five thousand animal species live in this biosphere reserve, which was named a UNESCO World Heritage Site in 1991.

The delta is home to a whopping 325 species of birds, including cormorants, silver egrets, terns, sea eagles and–the heraldic bird of the delta– pelicans, all of which either live here or at the least use it as a breeding, feeding or resting ground. And no wonder, with its fifty species of fish and vast

Moldawien gemeinsam widmen. Seit dem Jahr 2000 hat sich auch Bulgarien diesen Nationen angeschlossen, die nun gemeinsam die Renaturierung der gesamten unteren Donau vorantreiben.

Ein Vorhaben, das zumindest im Donaudelta sichtbare Früchte trägt. Es ist eine zauberhafte Region, die sich fortwährend verändert, wenn man sie nur lässt. Durch Sand und Kies, die die Donau mit sich trägt, und die Strömungen des Flusses entstehen neue Inseln, verlanden alte Kanäle und bilden sich andere an neuer Stelle. Das Donauwasser findet immer seinen Weg zum Schwarzen Meer. Doch zwischen dem Donauwasser gibt es immer wieder auch echtes Festland. Auf ihm liegen Städtchen wie Izmail – eine ehemalige türkische Festung – in der Ukraine oder zwischen dem Chilia- und Sulina-Arm der Urwald Letea mit seinem einmaligen Baumbestand aus Eschen, Erlen und Pappeln, mit Wildschweinen,

expanses of reeds, at 18,000 hectares (44,460 acres) the largest in the world. The delta is a natural paradise that Romania, Ukraine and Moldova have pledged to protect. In 2000 Bulgaria joined this group of nations that jointly promote the restoration of the entire Lower Danube Region.

This plan has been visibly fruitful, at least in the Danube delta. It is a magical region that changes continually when left to its own devices. The sand and gravel carried along by the Danube in combination with the river's currents form new islands, silt up old channels and form new ones elsewhere. The waters of the Danube always find their way to the Black Sea. But amidst the waters of the Danube there are also genuine landmasses, where one finds towns such as Izmail, a former Turkish fortress, in the Ukraine, or the Letea Forest located between the Chilia and Sulina branches. The forest boasts unique stands of ash, alder and poplar trees that

▾ Das Donaudelta nennt die größte Schilflandschaft der Welt sein Eigen.
▾ The Danube delta can claim the largest area of reed marshes in the world.

▾ Galeriewälder säumen teilweise die Ufer im Delta.
▾ Riparian forests line the riverbanks in parts of the delta.

Wölfen, Füchsen, Wildkatzen, Iltissen und Hasen und seinen Herden wilder Pferde, die man mit etwas Glück beobachten kann.

Und so darf sich die Donau nach über 2000 Kilometern, in denen sie mal mehr, mal weniger stark in ein von Menschenhand vorgeschriebenes Bett eingezwängt war, nun endlich ausbreiten, sich dehnen und strecken und in einem sehr natürlichen Verlauf bei Vylkove (mit dem Chilia-Arm), bei Sfantu George und bei Sulina ins Schwarze Meer fließen. Sie hat ihren Zweck erfüllt, hat Tausenden von Tier- und Pflanzenarten einen Lebensraum geschenkt, Felder bewässert und Weinberge klimatisiert, als internationale Wasserstraße gedient sowie Städten und Landschaften eine anmutige Würde verliehen.

Vor allem aber hat sie zehn europäische Nationen zusammengefügt, hat Millionen von Menschen gemeinsame Geschichte und Erinnerungen geschenkt und hinterlässt ihnen das Gefühl von Verbundenheit und Vertrautheit.

- Am alten Leuchtturm von Sulina vorbei fließt die Donau endlich ins Schwarze Meer.
- The Danube finally flows past the old lighthouse at Sulina into the Black Sea.

are home to wild boar, wolves, foxes, wildcats, polecats, rabbits and herds of wild horses that you might glimpse with a bit of luck.

And now, after more than 2,000 km (1,242 miles) in which she was confined in manmade riverbeds, sometimes to a greater extent and sometimes less, the Danube can finally stretch and spread out, and flow in a very natural progression past Vylkove on the Chilia branch, Sfantu Gheorghe and Sulina into the Black Sea. She has fulfilled her purpose, providing habitat for thousands of plant and animal species, irrigating fields and climatizing vineyards, serving as an international waterway, and lending a graceful dignity to towns, cities and landscapes.

Above all, she has brought ten European nations together, giving millions of people the gift of a common history and experience, leaving them with a feeling of familiarity and connection.

Abbildungsnachweis/Picture Credits

Umschlagabbildungen:

Vorderseite:
oben: iStockphoto.com, unten links: Inga Menkhoff, Mitte oben: BigStockPhoto.com, Mitte unten: BigStockPhoto.com, unten rechts: iStockphoto.com

Rückseite:
oben: iStockphoto.com, unten: istockphoto.com

BigStockPhoto.com: S. 47, 86, 95 oben links, 97 unten rechts, 98 unten rechts, 114, 115, 117, 119, 127, 131, 132, 133, 137, 138 oben links

Fotolia.com: S. 11: Alexis Borg, 15 unten links: henryart, 19: by-studio, 30: Vieraugen, 40: Sonne Fleckl, 42: Ornithologe82, 46: MajusCOOL, 52: Kawa, 60: fotofrank, 61: Walter Luger, 68: Digitalpress, 78: Digitalpress, 79: Peter Wienerroither, 85: nicolasjoseschirado, 110/111: Stanisa Martinovic, 112: Stanisa Martinovic, 139 unten rechts: Udo Kruse

Jutta Gay (Köln): S. 10, 18, 21 unten links, 21 unten rechts, 25, 26 oben links, 82, 88, 99 unten links, 99 unten rechts, 101 unten links, 107, 122, 126 unten links, 138 oben rechts

iStockphoto.com: S. 12 oben rechts, 14, 22/23, 24, 29, 31, 32, 33, 34, 35, 36, 37, 38/39, 41 unten links, 44, 45, 48/49, 53, 54/55, 58 unten links, 58 unten rechts, 62/63, 64, 65, 66 oben links, 69, 70, 71, 72/73, 74, 75, 76 unten links, 76 unten rechts, 77 unten links, 77 unten rechts, 83, 84, 87, 89, 90, 91, 92/93, 94, 95 oben rechts, 96, 101 unten rechts, 102, 103, 104/105, 106, 108, 109, 113, 116, 118, 120 unten links, 120 unten rechts, 121 oben links, 121 oben rechts, 123, 124/125, 126 unten rechts, 128, 129, 130, 134, 135, 136, 139 unten links, 141 unten rechts, 141 unten links, 142/143

mauritius images GmbH (Mittenwald): S. 56: Wolfgang Weinhäuptl, 100: Firstlight

Inga Menkhoff (Köln): S. 8, 9, 12 oben links, 13, 15 unten rechts, 16, 17, 20, 26, 27 oben rechts, 28 oben links, 28 oben rechts, 41 unten rechts, 43, 50, 51, 59, 66 oben rechts, 67 unten links, 67 unten rechts, 80 unten links, 80 unten rechts, 81 oben links, 81 oben rechts, 97 unten links, 98 unten links, 140

Karten Vor- und Nachsatz: Kartographie Huber, München

GERMANY
CZECH REPUBLIK
FRANCE
Rhein
Regensburg
Bavarian Forest
Bohemian Forest
Morava
Malé Karpaty
Ingolstadt
Danube
Strasbourg
Passau
Linz
Vienna
Bratislava
Ulm
Alpine Foreland
Inn
Neusiedler See
Esztergo
Breg
Brigach
Donau-eschingen
Freiburg
Chiem-see
Lake Constance
Lake Zürich
LIECHTEN-STEIN
Innsbruck
AUSTRIA
Rába
Bakon
Berne
SWITZERLAND
Alps
Balaton
SLOVENIA
Drava
Dolomites
Trento
Ljubljana
Zagreb
CROATIA
Lake Garda
Milan
Sava
Po
BOSNIA
HERZEGOV
ITALY
Sara
Firenze
SAN MARINO
Adriatic Sea
Split
Ligurian Sea